MasterChef
AUSTRALIA
SERIES 3

THE COOKBOOK

HarperCollins*Publishers*

Contents

Winner's foreword

When I naively walked through the doors of the MasterChef kitchen with 23 other contestants, I had no idea that I would one day walk out with the title 'MasterChef 2011'. While I might enjoy the honour of the title, none of us came away empty-handed. We have all shared an experience that has changed each of us, no matter how long that experience lasted.

We were immersed in a world of food – complete with world-renowned chefs, the best Australian produce and judges who genuinely wanted to see us grow – and that has equipped us to follow our dreams and make the most of our love of food.

One of the things that surprised me most about MasterChef was the rich resource the contestants found in each other. Not only did our common interest in food bring us together, but we were bonded by the once-in-a-lifetime experiences we enjoyed together. Life-long friendships have been cemented and the sharing of our food histories taught us more about each other than we could ever have imagined.

I discovered so much about Asian cuisine from Dani; I learnt how to make curry from Kumar; I tasted my first foie gras courtesy of Mat; and I learnt a little about the world of molecular gastronomy from Danielle.

Peter showed me that it's never too late to try something new; Billy taught me that pressure doesn't need to get you down; Alana demonstrated that quiet determination gets you a long way; Hayden showed me the value of disciplined study; Ellie taught me the value of never giving up; and Michael proved that competitors can be great mates, too.

The recipes in this book reflect so much more than just food on a plate – they tell the stories of our lives for the months we shared. They also reflect our common desire to put a smile on the face of whoever was eating: the slowly emerging smile under glittering eyes from Matt Preston; the grin from George as he'd turn silently to beckon the other judges to come and enjoy a mouthful, too; the smile around the second lick of the spoon from Gary; or the explosive beam that comes immediately to Matt Moran – these were the smiles we all enjoyed most in the MasterChef kitchen.

But the smiles in the house were equally enthralling: Ellie's grin on seeing the array of canapés set out for her 21st birthday; the joy in people's steps when they smelt that Jay was cooking pork crackling again; the delight when Mat put down a perfectly cooked venison with faultless cauliflower purée for our first dinner party; the fun of two birthday cakes when Rachel and Michael had a combined 70th birthday; and the excitement when the final seven sat down to our own creation of a seven-course dégustation dinner.

But, even without the food, we enjoyed countless conversations outside as we took in the view; we learnt of previously unknown singing abilities through SingStar; we laughed ourselves silly with charades;

we shared jokes and tears and cookbooks. And Rachel and I ended every day with a cup of tea on the back step.

These high points made all the stress and struggle worthwhile. Of course, we dealt with bucketloads of pressure, we missed our families and friends immeasurably, and we persevered through sleepless nights and gut-wrenching anxiety. But, for all that toil and heartache, we emerged stronger, more focused on our goals and more fearless than we'd ever been before.

We rose (quite literally at times) to the challenges presented to us, both in the kitchen and in the sheer fact that we were away from our normal lives. In doing so, we learnt so much and cooked in some incredible places: a remote gold mine in Western Australia, Cronulla beach, a pop-up restaurant at Circular Quay, the Moran family farm, and in every nook and cranny of New York. And we cooked for some of the biggest names in the culinary world: Heston Blumenthal, Thomas Keller, Andoni Aduriz, Marco Pierre White, David Chang, Nigella Lawson, Maggie Beer and, for Michael and me, René Redzepi.

And the beautiful fact is that so many of you shared it with us. We may not have seen you or known your names, but we knew you were there. And our hope is that, as you cook the recipes in this book, you, too, will relive the joy of MasterChef.

I feel incredibly blessed to have been a part of this series and the MasterChef family and I know that for years to come I'll remain thankful for the people I met, the experiences I had and the food I tasted – both in front of the camera and behind it.

Thank you for sharing the journey with us.

Kate Bracks
Australia's MasterChef 2011

The Top 24

ADAM *Bowen*

About: Scuba diving instructor; 30; Brisbane, QLD
Personality: 'I'm not one to lose, and I don't like failure.'
Can tickle a shark to sleep but found presenting a
plate of food to the MasterChef judges intimidating.
Defining moment: Listening to Danielle talk about her
passion to stay after week 8's elimination test with
Mary Calombaris, and realising that 'I didn't need my
life to be changed'; he already had a career he loved.

ALANA *Lowes*

About: Journalist; 30; Brisbane, QLD
Personality: Calm – most successful team captain.
Finest hour: Creating a near-perfect Corton gold bar
dessert in New York with Ellie; Winning the 'cook for
someone you love' challenge and going home to
dinner served by the judges; Third place MasterChef.
Darkest day: The 'evil Zumbo gingerbread house'.
Now: Writes food and travel blog, 'a morish distraction'.

ALEX *Glasson*

About: Mining machinist; 27; Perth, WA
Personality: Enthusiastic, passionate, talented,
tattooed, risk-taker, summed up by Matt Preston: 'In
your short time here you've lit up the place.'
Best TV moment: Rolling out from under a car to find
Matt Moran with a wild card into the Top 24; Finessing
the meringue on his elimination bombe Alaska, while
Gary screamed: 'You're not Picasso! Get the stuff on!'
Now: Working to find a chef's apprenticeship.

ANDREW *Henderson*

About: Youth worker; 37; Port Lincoln, SA
Personality: Gentle, but with a firm core: 'If you want
something bad enough, fight for it.' Drew strength in
challenges from his dream of opening a bistro and
cookery training school for disadvantaged kids.
Darkest day: Captaining the losing boys' team at the
Mean Fiddler; The massaman curry elimination against
Kumar: 'My brain melted under the pressure.'

ARENA *Dunn*

About: Personal trainer; 25; Perth, WA
Personality: Fitness and organic food fanatic, even at school: 'I gravitate towards veggies, as it's all I've ever really known.' Loves classical and stage singing.
Finest hour: Being on the winning team at Cronulla Beach and running into the ocean fully clothed.
Now: Runs the family business, Absolutely Organic, in Gwelup, WA, with boyfriend Travis.

BILLY *Law*

About: Web designer; 34; Central Coast, NSW
Known for: Contestants' favourite to take the title.
Finest hour: Winning the 'down on the farm' challenge; Exploring the Bronx; Cooking pork belly – George's 'dish of the series' – with Marco Pierre White; Quoting Cher lyrics to Peter before his elimination challenge.
Darkest day: Making 'green soup' at the UN.
Now: Writes food blog, 'a table for two'; Hosts 'Just Desserts' dinner events; Plans to open a dessert bar.

CHELSEA *Fammartino*

About: Retail manager; 34; Melbourne, VIC
Best TV moment: Showing steadfast loyalty when Alex dropped the cake in the Maggie Beer pressure test: 'I'm not going to let him serve up nothing.'
Darkest day: Smoking octopus; Competing against her two best friends in the Chinese elimination test.
Now: Working in Lygon Street restaurant Donnini's; Holds cooking classes with her father, Rocco.

CLEO *Kerameas*

About: Executive assistant; 45; Sydney, NSW
Finest hour: Being in the top two, with Jay, for her rabbit mystery box dish – she'd cooked rabbit with her mother, Eva, who lost her battle with cancer after encouraging Cleo to apply for the show.
Darkest day: Multi-tasking and being eliminated even though she put up a great dessert.
Now: 'Cleo's Food' catering and cooking classes.

CRAIG *Young*

About: Professional musician; 43; Brisbane, QLD
Best TV moment: Racing into the MasterChef kitchen garden with seconds to spare to find sprigs of rosemary for his 'William Tell' apple fritters.
Finest hour: Cooking Heston's burger and fries.
Most hated challenge: 'Canned and frozen' in week 5.
Now: Working on 'musical menus' website and book; Attending a Fiji food festival as guest cook and cellist.

DANI *Venn*

About: Publicist; 25; Melbourne, VIC
Personality: Glass-half-full, heart-on-her-sleeve, bubbly, bubbly and more bubbly... even when crying.
Finest hour: Impressing David Chang with her Korean rice burger; Creating the frozen baklava; Cooking for the Dalai Lama; Winning immunity twice; Fourth place.
Darkest day: Making chocolate lollipops at the UN.
Now: Blogs at danivenn.com; Plans to open her own Asian food store in Melbourne.

DANIELLE *Dixon*

About: Administrative manager in the family car mechanic business; 29; Brisbane, QLD
Known for: 1950s rockabilly fashion and retro food.
Finest hour: Winning the tricky Spanish invention test; Winning Neil Perry's Qantas challenge with Kate and punching her in the arm in excitement.
Darkest day: Making gnocchi on an open fire in the rain.
Now: Blogs at danielledixon.com.au; Apprenticeships at Rockpool and Quay; 'Dinner with Danielle' catering.

ELLIE *Paxton-Hall*

About: Student nurse; 21; Brisbane, QLD
Known for: Saved herself in five pressure tests and nicknamed the 'Ellie-minator' by the other contestants; The season's youngest competitor – celebrated her 21st birthday in the house; Messy in the kitchen!
Finest hour: Week 11 in New York and winning immunity in Central Park; A spectacular bombe Alaska.
Darkest day: The Spanish invention test – Gary described her capsicum as 'strangely unpleasant'.
Now: Working at Rockpool Bar & Grill, Melbourne.

HAYDEN *Quinn*

About: Professional lifeguard; 24; Sydney, NSW
Known for: The viewers' tip to win when Jay was eliminated, but only ever won one team challenge.
Finest hour: Surprising David Chang with his pork belly: 'I didn't see that coming from you'; Winning immunity against Ormeggio apprentice, Alex; Helping Michael make sense of Heston's five-page burger recipe from the balcony: 'Mate, I'm under the pump here!'
Now: Showcases recipes at haydenquinn.com.au; Negotiating forthcoming cookbook and TV show.

JAY *Huxley*

About: Car sales manager; 31; Sydney, NSW
Best TV quote: 'I've never bought a sausage sandwich because of a guy in his swimmers,' – aimed at Hayden in his Cronulla budgie smugglers.
Finest hour: The whole of week 5 in WA; Creating his 'garden of marron' and cooking twice for immunity.
Now: Securing a spot in Sydney's restaurant scene; Work experience with Colin Fassnidge and Dan Hong.

KATE *Bracks*

About: Mother of three; 36; Orange, NSW
Best TV moment: Seeing husband Luke and their children, Erin, Liam and Maya, arrive for the 'cook for someone you love' challenge.
Finest hour: Making 'retro coffee cake'; Bringing Gary to his knees with her version of Darren Purchese's dessert; Creating her own dessert at Quay.
Now: MasterChef 2011; Planning Orange's first 'foodie' bed & breakfast; Writing a dessert cookbook.

KUMAR *Pereira*

About: Design teacher; 62; Sydney, NSW
Best TV quote: 'Do you deserve to be in the Top 24 more than Seamus?' asked George, with Kumar and Seamus nervous in front of him. 'As well as,' said Kumar, pointedly. 'You're a nice man,' George told him.
Darkest day: Running across Jim Moran's farm with a lamb carcass; The elimination blindfold taste test.
Now: Working on recipe sheets with his own beautiful illustrations; Leading culinary tours of Sri Lanka.

MAT *Beyer*

About: IT tech support; 24; Melbourne, VIC
Finest hour: Meeting his hero, David Chang, and hearing him praise his 'Korean carpaccio'.
Darkest day: Cooking the steaks at the Mean Fiddler challenge; Being left to make Yorkshire puddings for Nigella Lawson, without a recipe; Leaving the show because he had a mobile phone in his possession.
Best TV moment: Gary's phone ringing during the reunion masterclass: 'Mat, it's for you!'

MICHAEL *Weldon*

About: Film projectionist; 25; Adelaide, SA
Best TV quote: On Michael's reaching week 13 without a chance to cook for immunity, George asked: 'Is there a cupboard full of bridesmaids' dresses in your room?'
Finest hour: Serving a burger and shake to Heston in memory of his father; Being paid for his 43rd Street taco; Cooking venison at est.; Runner-up MasterChef.
Darkest day: Being pitted against Hayden in week 12's elimination test and sending his best mate home.
Best TV moment: Doing a mad little dance on hearing he's in the finals. 'Give it a bit, Michael!' shouted George.
Now: Apprenticeship at Gary Mehigan's Fenix.

PETER *Vickery*

About: Account manager; 50; Sydney, NSW
Best TV moment: Happily cooking marinated lamb over an open fire at the Moran family farm. The judges loved his dish – Matt Moran wanted the recipe – but he ended up in the bottom 3. 'Farmers don't eat couscous, mate,' Jim Moran comforted him.
Now: Moved to the Hunter Valley; Creating kitchen gardens and blogging at cityboynomore.com.

RACHEL *McSweeney*

About: Mum, office administrator; 45; Perth, WA
Finest hour: Pulling the Gen X team to victory with Kate and the chocolate cake Nigella Lawson loved.
Darkest day: Getting her meats muddled as she made Heston's 'perfection burger' in the elimination test: 'When I saw Heston, I thought, "That's it, I'm going".'
Now: Pursuing a career as a functions coordinator.

SEAMUS *Ashley*

About: Graphic and web designer; 32; Melbourne, VIC
Known for: Love of Japanese-style cooking.
Finest hour: Taking a risk in the Top 50 'cook your catch' elimination challenge, and hauling in the fish.
Darkest day: Elimination when he took his eye off his stir-fry sauce during the 'rapid-fire' boys' challenge.
Now: Hopes to work on restaurant websites and blogs.

SHANNON *Smyth*

About: Receptionist; 26; Gold Coast, QLD
Known for: Winning over fiancé, Shane, with a gourmet lunch after they met at a real estate course.
Finest hour: Meeting Nigella Lawson, a personal hero; Her elimination French toast, which sadly came up against Craig's equally stunning Thai prawns.
Now: Applying for chef apprenticeship positions; Hopes to one day open a florist–pâtisserie.

SUN *Etheridge*

About: Credit analyst; 32; Brisbane, QLD
Known for: Brought up as a Hari Krishna vegetarian and discovered her inner carnivore in Paris in 2009.
Finest hour: Winning every team challenge, twice as captain, even when disaster seemed imminent; Creating the 'pig in a bag' with Craig and Peter.
Darkest day: Spending New York week in lockdown after disaster with her art gallery-inspired cake; Not noticing there were four cooks and only three deep-fryers in Sylvia's Soul Food Restaurant.
Now: Pursuing a career in food media.

TOM *Rutledge*

About: General manager; 29; Sydney, NSW
Finest hour: Proving himself a great team leader in the Sonoma bakery challenge, but losing regardless.
Darkest day: Stepping up as captain to volunteer for elimination when his team lost – 'Don't hold back,' he told Kumar; Being the first elimination of Series 3.
Now: Running an internet-based gourmet home-delivery store, mrperkins.com.au, selling local seasonal produce and precisely weighed small quantities of 'obscure ingredients' needed for recipes.

THE TOP 50

The Top 50 are on Cockatoo Island to cook to change their lives and win the 24 white MasterChef aprons. A giant mystery box is lowered by helicopter, Adriano Zumbo scares everyone with a cloche full of chocolate, Matt Moran puts the boot in and Maggie Beer hands out hugs. By the end of the week, 12 contestants are wearing white aprons.

FILMING DIARY

Sunday

EPISODE 1 Is it a bird? Is it a plane? No, it's the mother of all mystery boxes.

Monday

EPISODE 2 Forty-five hopefuls get back to basics in Matt Moran's boot camp.

Tuesday

EPISODE 3 The Maggie Beer pressure test sees Alex in trouble again.

Wednesday

EPISODE 4 A day for risks... To go fishing and catch something fantastic – or not?

Thursday

EPISODE 5 The contestants are all washed up on a desert island.

Friday

EPISODE 6 Time out from the stress to enjoy the first masterclass of the season.

Week 1

THE GIANT MYSTERY BOX

A giant mystery box is lowered onto Cockatoo Island by helicopter. What's in the crate? Nick thinks it might be a live cow. Hayden (already showing a horror of desserts) is scared it's an oven and a cupcake tin. A rumour goes around that it's Donna Hay.

The ingredients are everyday and meatballs are everywhere. It's all harder than it looks and, before she knows it, Sun is plating up 'a dish of oil and butter'. The top 4 in this very first challenge are Alana, Peter, Michael and Kate... sound familiar?

In Turbine Hall, the bottom 10 have to cook with chocolate for Adriano Zumbo. Rather worryingly, he doesn't want to see 'your grandma's chocolate cake, or mousse in a cup'. Alex redeems himself with crème brûlées that make Adriano shake his hand and Matt Preston say 'awesome' for the first time in his life.

Below: A 'joint effort' is what Chelsea and Alex call their pressure test. A 'collaboration' is what the judges call it. Alex drops one of their cakes and George's jaw drops too.

GONE FISHIN'

Four contestants take the risk to head out to sea in a boat to catch their 'elimination protein'. The others take the risk to cook with whatever's lurking under the judges' cloche. By the time the boat gets back the cloche has filled them with terror... what's under there? Is it tripe? Brains? No, it's crocodile. John has a much better day and serves up the best-cooked croc.

DESERT ISLAND DINNER

If you were washed up on a desert island, what would you want to eat for eternity? Billy's pork belly and Alana's chocolate puddings are what the judges would choose. By the end of the day, there are 12 contestants with white aprons. 'They're like the Holy Grail,' says Danielle.

Clockwise from below: 'I've never caught a fish in my life, but I'm feeling lucky today,' says Seamus, when he chooses the fishing option in the elimination test; Kumar cooks up a prawn curry to eat on a desert island and gets himself an apron; Seamus catches enough fish 'to feed 10 people'.

The judges take the 'desert island' challenge very seriously.

BOOTCAMP BOTHER

After three rounds of Matt Moran's 'bootcamp basic skills' challenge, peeling potatoes and cutting up chickens, Sun and Alex find themselves making scones in another elimination test. George and Matt M wonder if Alex's tactic is to get more experience by cooking twice as much as everyone else.

JOHN STUNS THE JUDGES

The Top 40 face a Maggie Beer dessert pressure test that will give six of them MasterChef aprons. The contestants are to share ovens but some get carried away and start baking together. Alex is in trouble again, this time for cooking with Chelsea. To add to the drama he sets fire to his bag of sugar. Meanwhile, John has decided he's not happy with his dishes and declines to bring them to tasting.

Serves **4**
Preparation **20 minutes**
Cooking **12 minutes**

Alana's
STUFFED TOMATOES WITH
BUTTERY MINT PEAS

The giant mystery box contained ordinary ingredients – the challenge was to turn them into something extraordinary. Alana's stuffed tomatoes were George's first 'cracker dish'. Their clean fresh taste got Alana the first high-five of the series from Gary.

4 large ripe truss tomatoes
1 tbs olive oil
4 rashers rindless bacon, finely chopped
Extra virgin olive oil and lemon juice, to drizzle

STUFFING
2 tbs butter
1 onion, finely chopped
1 clove garlic, crushed
2 large flat mushrooms, finely chopped

Zest of ½ lemon in wide strips
BUTTERY MINT PEAS
20g butter
240g (2 cups) frozen peas
24 mint leaves
1 tsp lemon zest

1 Bring a large saucepan of water to the boil. Score a cross in the skin at the base of each tomato, then blanch in boiling water for 20 seconds. Lift out and refresh immediately in a bowl of iced water. Cool, then peel away skins from tomatoes. Cut off the tops (keeping the stem intact if you can) and scoop out the seeds.

2 **To make stuffing,** melt butter in a large frying pan over high heat and cook onion, garlic and mushrooms for 4 minutes or until onion is soft. Add lemon peel, season with salt and pepper and cook for a further 2 minutes. Remove from heat and discard lemon peel.

3 **To make buttery mint peas,** melt butter in a frying pan over medium heat. Add peas, season with salt and pepper and cook for 3 minutes or until peas are warmed through. Remove from heat and stir in mint leaves and lemon zest to taste.

4 Meanwhile, heat oil in a large frying pan over high heat, add bacon and cook for 3 minutes or until crisp. Drain on paper towel.

5 Spoon stuffing into tomatoes, top with a little crisp bacon and replace tomato lid. Serve with peas, a drizzle of extra virgin olive oil and a little lemon juice squeezed over.

Serves **4**
Preparation **35 minutes**
Cooking **40 minutes**

Peter's
MINESTRONE WITH SPAETZLE
& MINT GREMOLATA

'This is a really top dish,' said George when he tasted Peter's minestrone. Much later in the series we found out that if Peter wasn't an account manager he'd like to be a farmer and this rustic dish summed up his style of cooking from the very first. It's simple to make and uses every bit of the vegetables – true farmhouse fare.

SPAETZLE
200g (1¹/₃ cups) plain flour
1 tbs extra virgin olive oil
2 eggs, lightly beaten
BROTH
5 rashers bacon
2 desiree potatoes, washed

2 large flat mushrooms
4 tomatoes, chopped
120g (1 cup) peas
2 tbs extra virgin olive oil
2 onions, chopped
4 cloves garlic, chopped
1L (4 cups) vegetable stock

MINT GREMOLATA
Zest of ¹/₂ lemon, cut into julienne
³/₄ cup chopped mint leaves
3 cloves garlic, finely diced
1 tbs extra virgin olive oil

1 **To make spaetzle,** combine flour and a pinch of salt in a mixing bowl and make a well in the centre. Add oil, eggs and about 1 tablespoon water or enough to make a soft dough. Work in the flour with your hand. Turn onto a lightly floured work surface and knead for 2 minutes until smooth. Wrap in plastic wrap and leave for 30 minutes.

2 **Meanwhile, to make broth,** cut rind and fat from bacon and set aside. Keep 2 rashers bacon aside and finely chop the rest. Peel potatoes and keep the peel; cut potatoes into 1cm cubes. Peel mushrooms and keep the stalks; chop mushroom caps. Remove core and seeds from tomatoes and keep; chop tomato flesh.

3 Heat olive oil in a saucepan over medium–high heat and cook onion and garlic for 3 minutes or until soft. Add bacon rind and chopped bacon and cook for 5 minutes. Reduce heat to medium and add chopped potato, mushroom, tomatoes and peas. Cook for 7 minutes or until softened; lift out the bacon rind.

4 Meanwhile, put the vegetable peelings and trimmings, stock, bacon rind and remaining bacon in a saucepan. Bring to the boil, reduce heat and simmer for 10 minutes. Strain, then measure 250ml (1 cup) and pour over the softened vegetables. Keep the rest of the broth warm.

5 **To make mint gremolata,** mix together all ingredients and season with salt and pepper.

6 Take pinches (about ¹/₄ tsp each) of the spaetzle dough and rub between your fingers into thin 2cm lengths. Dust with flour. Bring the remaining broth to the boil and cook the spaetzle in small batches for 3 minutes or until tender.

7 Scatter cooked vegetables and spaetzle into serving bowls, ladle the broth into the bowls and top with gremolata.

Rachel's
BEST BROWNIES WITH CHOCOLATE SAUCE

Rachel's meatballs (although cunningly disguised as 'beef bites') put her in the bottom 10 of the mystery box challenge, leaving her cooking for renowned MasterChef torturer Adriano Zumbo in Turbine Hall. She was confident her favourite brownie recipe would win him over, and she was right: 'Adriano Zumbo likes the brownies,' he said with a grin.

150g unsalted butter, chopped
125g dark chocolate (70% cocoa
  solids), chopped
3 eggs
1 tsp vanilla extract

330g (1½ cups) caster sugar
150g (1 cup) plain flour
25g (¼ cup) dark (Dutch) cocoa
Raspberries, blueberries and
  vanilla ice-cream, to serve

CHOCOLATE SAUCE
50ml cream
180g dark chocolate (70% cocoa
  solids), chopped

1 Preheat oven to 170°C. Grease a 20cm round cake pan and line base with baking paper. Fill a small saucepan one-third full with water and bring to a gentle simmer. Put butter and chocolate in a small heatproof bowl, place over pan and stir until melted (don't let the bowl touch the water). Stir until smooth, transfer to a mixing bowl and cool slightly.
2 Add eggs to chocolate one at a time, beating well after each addition. Stir in vanilla, sugar, sifted flour and cocoa powder.
3 Pour into cake pan and bake for 30 minutes or until slightly risen in the centre and just firm when touched. Leave to cool in pan (it will sink and flatten).
4 **To make chocolate sauce,** pour cream into a small saucepan and bring to simmer over medium heat. Place chocolate in a small heatproof bowl, pour hot cream over the chocolate and stir gently until chocolate has melted.
5 Cut brownies into wedges and serve with chocolate sauce, berries and ice-cream.

Chef Maggie Beer's
OLIVE OIL, ROSEMARY & APPLE PUDDING

Although it was a pressure test, Maggie Beer was met with rapturous applause from the contestants. 'The whole room just lit up when she appeared. It was like sunshine coming in,' said Cleo. Cellist Craig was given a MasterChef apron as soon as the judges tasted this cake. Michael, Kate, Hayden, Adam and Cleo all joined him in the Top 24.

POACHED APPLES
4 large pink lady apples, peeled, cored, each cut into 8 wedges
300ml verjuice
1 tbs finely chopped rosemary
1 tbs extra virgin olive oil

OLIVE OIL PUDDING
3 eggs, separated
125g caster sugar
75g (1/2 cup) plain flour
1/2 tsp baking powder
60ml (1/4 cup) extra virgin olive oil

GLAZE
55g (1/4 cup) caster sugar
SABAYON
2 egg yolks
1 tsp caster sugar

1 Preheat oven to 190°C. Grease a 20cm springform pan and line the base with baking paper.
2 **To make poached apples,** put apples, verjuice and rosemary in a large deep frying pan. Cover and bring to the boil over high heat.
3 Reduce heat to low and simmer, covered, for 8 minutes or until tender. Remove apples from heat and strain, keeping the liquid. Set 1 1/2 tbs liquid aside for the sabayon. Return apples to frying pan over high heat. Add olive oil and cook, turning occasionally, for 5 minutes or until apples start to colour. Remove from heat and arrange in base of springform pan.
4 **To make olive oil pudding,** use electric beaters to beat egg whites in a small bowl until soft peaks form. Gradually add half the sugar and beat until dissolved.
5 In a separate bowl, beat yolks and remaining sugar until pale. Sift in flour and baking powder, pour in oil and 60ml (1/4 cup) apple poaching liquid. Stir gently, then fold in the meringue in three batches until just combined.
6 Pour into springform pan over apples and bake for 35 minutes or until pudding springs back to the touch; cover loosely with foil after 10 minutes if browning too quickly. Remove from oven and cool in pan for 5 minutes. Release sides of pan and turn out onto a wire rack to cool.
7 **For glaze,** put sugar and remaining poaching liquid into a small saucepan. Stir over medium heat without boiling until sugar has dissolved. Bring to the boil. Reduce heat to low and simmer for 4 minutes or until reduced by half.
8 **To make sabayon,** fill a saucepan one-third full with water and bring to a gentle simmer. Place egg yolks, sugar and the 1 1/2 tbs poaching liquid in a heatproof bowl and place over the pan (don't let the bowl touch the water). Whisk vigorously until the mixture is pale and frothy. Cook, whisking continuously, for 5 minutes or until cooked. To test, drizzle a figure-of-eight trail of sabayon from the whisk; when it holds its shape it is ready. Remove from heat and whisk until cool. Pour into a serving jug.
9 Brush pudding with the glaze and cut into thick wedges. Serve with sabayon.

Serves **6**
Preparation **30 minutes**
Cooking **20 minutes**

Chef Maggie Beer's
LEMON CURD TARTS

This sour cream pastry is very simple, yet it's so crisp and short that it really does melt in the mouth. Remember Maggie's advice – rest the pastry, chill it and don't overwork it. The lemon curd is covered with sugar and blowtorched for a crisp crust. Kitchen blowtorches are handy and inexpensive, but if you don't have one just fill with lemon curd and serve.

120g (³/4 cup) icing sugar, to dust

LEMON CURD

4 egg yolks

75g (¹/3 cup) caster sugar

3 tsp lemon zest

80ml (¹/3 cup) lemon juice, strained

40g unsalted butter, chopped

SOUR CREAM PASTRY

150g (1 cup) plain flour

60g unsalted butter, chopped

60g sour cream

1 Preheat oven to 190°C. Lightly grease six 7cm tart pans with removable bases.

2 **To make lemon curd,** whisk yolks and sugar in a small saucepan until pale. Add lemon zest, juice and butter and place over very low heat. Cook, whisking continuously, for 7 minutes or until curd coats the back of a spoon. Strain into a bowl and cool slightly, stirring to release the heat. Cover the surface with plastic wrap and leave to cool.

3 **To make pastry,** process flour and butter in a food processor until mixture resembles crumbs. Add sour cream and process until mixture just comes together. Divide dough into 6 portions and shape into discs. Wrap in plastic and refrigerate for 10 minutes.

4 Place each pastry disc between two sheets of baking paper and roll out to fit pans. Gently ease into pans and trim away excess pastry. Refrigerate for 10 minutes. Prick bases with a fork. Line with baking paper and fill with baking beads, dried beans or rice. Bake for 10 minutes, then remove beads and paper and bake for 5 minutes or until crisp and golden. Cool on a wire rack.

5 Fill with lemon curd and dust generously with icing sugar. Using a blowtorch, gently heat the icing sugar until golden and caramelised. Dust and caramelise twice more for a crisp crust.

Winemaker John likes to work at his own pace and wasn't happy with his dishes. He wouldn't even let the judges taste, preferring to go straight into an elimination test. He got a hug from Maggie for his integrity.

Nick's
SLOW-ROASTED BREAM IN WHITE WINE WITH DILL & PARSLEY BUTTER

Nick Kulakoff loves fishing, so he was thrilled to head out to sea on a boat for the risky 'cook your catch' elimination challenge. In the end he didn't make it into the Top 24, but his fish dish took out the honours in this challenge. 'The flavours are great, you've cooked everything very well and this is one of the best things we've tasted,' said Matt Preston.

8 deep-sea bream fillets*
500ml (2 cups) dry white wine
2 lemons, thickly sliced
2 bunches asparagus, trimmed
Chives and extra lemon slices,
  to serve
DILL & PARSLEY BUTTER
200g butter, softened
100g crème fraîche*

¼ cup finely chopped flat-leaf
  parsley
¼ cup finely chopped dill
½ lemon, juiced
DEVILLED EGGS
4 eggs
50g crème fraîche
1 tsp finely chopped parsley
1 tsp finely chopped dill

2 tsp lemon juice
GARLIC BREAD
50g butter, softened
2 cloves garlic, crushed
4 slices ciabatta (about 3cm
  thick)
¼ cup chopped flat-leaf parsley

1 **To make dill and parsley butter,** preheat oven to 85°C. Beat together butter and crème fraîche until smooth. Beat in parsley, dill and lemon juice. Season with salt and pepper.
2 Arrange fish fillets in a single layer in a lightly greased deep ovenproof dish. Pour in wine and cover fish with lemon slices. Dot with 250g dill and parsley butter, keeping the rest to serve. Cover with foil and cook for 50 minutes or until fish flakes easily. Lift out fish, keeping juices.
3 **Meanwhile, to make devilled eggs,** place eggs in a saucepan half-filled with water. Bring to the boil over high heat, stirring the eggs to centre the yolks. Cook for 5 minutes, then plunge into iced water until cold.
4 Whisk the crème fraîche, parsley, dill and lemon juice in a small bowl. Peel eggs and cut in half lengthwise. Carefully scoop out yolks and mash into crème fraîche mixture, cover with plastic wrap and chill in fridge. Spoon into a piping bag fitted with a small nozzle, and pipe into the egg whites.
5 **To make garlic bread,** preheat grill to high. Mix butter and garlic together and spread over ciabatta slices. Grill until golden. Sprinkle with parsley.
6 Pour reserved pan juices into a saucepan and bring to the boil over high heat. Reduce heat to low and simmer until reduced by half.
7 Meanwhile, cook asparagus in boiling salted water for 2 minutes or until just tender.
8 Serve bream fillets with the pan juices, a little extra herbed butter, devilled eggs, asparagus and chives to garnish. Serve with extra lemon slices and garlic bread.

TIP **Deep-sea bream** is also sold as morwong. **Crème fraîche** is available from selected supermarkets and delis.

SOFT-HEARTED CHOCOLATE PUDDINGS WITH RASPBERRY CREAM & HONEYCOMB

Alana and Billy won their MasterChef aprons in the 'desert island' challenge. 'This dish must taste amazing, and it must represent who you are,' said George. Alana's gooey puddings with crunchy honeycomb chunks had the judges scraping the plate clean.

HONEYCOMB
365g caster sugar
140g liquid glucose*
1 tsp bicarbonate of soda
RASPBERRY CREAM
300ml thickened cream
2 tbs icing sugar
200g fresh or frozen raspberries, crushed

RASPBERRY ESSENCE
200g fresh or frozen raspberries, crushed
2 tbs caster sugar
4 strips lemon zest (about 2cm wide, white pith removed)
1 lemon, juiced
CHOCOLATE PUDDINGS
125g unsalted butter, chopped

150g dark chocolate (70% cocoa solids), chopped
2 eggs
2 egg yolks
125g caster sugar
1 tsp vanilla extract
50g ($1/3$ cup) self-raising flour
Fresh raspberries, to decorate

1 To make honeycomb, grease an 18 x 28cm slice pan and line with baking paper, leaving paper overhanging the long sides. Combine sugar, glucose and 125ml ($1/2$ cup) water in a large saucepan. Stir over medium heat without boiling until sugar has dissolved. Bring to the boil, reduce heat to low–medium and simmer for 8 minutes or until light golden. Remove from heat.

2 Add bicarbonate of soda and quickly whisk into the sugar syrup (it will froth and bubble). Pour immediately into slice pan (take care as pan will become very hot). Leave for 45 minutes until cool and hard. Break into small chunks.

3 To make raspberry cream, whisk together cream and icing sugar until soft peaks form. Fold in crushed raspberries and chill until required.

4 To make raspberry essence, combine all ingredients with 100ml water in a large saucepan. Stir over medium heat to dissolve sugar, then bring to the boil. Reduce heat and simmer for 5 minutes or until liquid is reduced and syrupy. Strain through muslin cloth into a jug.

5 To make chocolate puddings, preheat oven to 200°C. Grease six 150ml dariole moulds* and line bases with circles of baking paper. Place on an oven tray. Fill a small saucepan one-third full with water and bring to a gentle simmer. Place butter and chocolate in a small heatproof bowl over pan and stir until melted (don't let the bowl touch the water). Stir until smooth, remove bowl from pan and cool slightly.

6 Place eggs, yolks, sugar and vanilla in a bowl and whisk until thick and pale. Fold in flour until combined, then gently fold in chocolate mixture. Pour into moulds. Bake for 12 minutes or until risen and just set but still wobbly in the centre. Leave to cool for 5 minutes.

7 Run a knife around each pudding to loosen before turning out. Remove paper and serve puddings with raspberry cream, honeycomb, fresh raspberries and raspberry essence.

TIP **Liquid glucose** is available from health food shops and large supermarkets. **Dariole moulds** are small metal ramekins used for baking individual puddings.

'This is the dish of the day for me.'
Matt Preston

Serves **4-6**

Preparation **1½ hours + 2 hours chilling**

Cooking **1 hour 40 minutes**

Billy's
TWICE-COOKED PORK BELLY

Could you eat this for eternity? Gary certainly couldn't leave the crackling alone for long. This is Billy's mum's recipe – it's the first dish he learnt to make and it's still his favourite. The flavours are Malaysian and the richness of the pork belly is balanced with tangy apples, lemon and ginger. George had only four words to say to Billy: 'Dish of the day.'

1 kg piece pork belly

5 slices ginger

5 star anise

60ml (¼ cup) black vinegar

3 cloves garlic, peeled

100ml light soy sauce

60ml (¼ cup) kecap manis

110g (½ cup) caster sugar

2 tbs olive oil

40g (⅓ cup) sea salt flakes

150g (1 cup) cornflour

1 egg, lightly beaten

Vegetable oil, to deep-fry

APPLE SLAW

2 granny smith apples, unpeeled

2 tbs caster sugar

1 lemon, juiced

PAN-GRILLED RICE CAKES

200g (1 cup) jasmine rice, unrinsed

SWEET GINGER DRESSING

55g (¼ cup) sugar

2 tbs soy sauce

3cm piece ginger, grated

1 Cut off pork belly skin in one piece and set aside. Pat flesh dry with paper towel. Pour 2 litres water into a large saucepan. Add pork, ginger, star anise, vinegar and garlic. Bring to the boil, then boil for 5 minutes, skimming the surface occasionally. Add light soy sauce, kecap manis and sugar, reduce heat to low and simmer, uncovered, for 1½ hours or until pork is tender. Lift out and drain pork and cool slightly for 5 minutes. Reserve 500ml (2 cups) braising liquid.

2 Sandwich pork between two chopping boards weighted with cans. Refrigerate for 2 hours.

3 Meanwhile, preheat oven to 200°C. Score pork skin, lay flat on an oven tray and rub with oil. Pack top side of skin with sea salt. Bake for 20 minutes to render fat. Remove from the oven, pour fat into a bowl and set aside. Increase oven to 250°C. Brush salt from skin and return skin to oven. Roast for 30 minutes, checking every 10 minutes, or until skin is blistered and crunchy. Cool and cut into small pieces.

4 To make apple slaw, core and cut apples into julienne slices. Toss with sugar and lemon juice and leave for 30 minutes to pickle. Squeeze out excess liquid and set apple slaw aside.

5 To make rice cakes, simmer rice in water over low heat for 12 minutes or until tender; drain well. Spread over an oven tray to cool. Shape heaped tablespoonfuls of rice into cylinders.

6 Heat reserved pork fat in a large frying pan and cook rice cakes in two batches, rolling cakes in the pan, until crisp and golden. Remove and drain on paper towel.

7 For sweet ginger dressing, place sugar and soy sauce in a small saucepan over low heat and stir to dissolve. Bring to the boil over medium heat and cook for 2 minutes or until beginning to caramelise. Add the 500ml reserved braising liquid and bring to the boil. Reduce heat to low and simmer for 10 minutes or until reduced by half. Remove from heat, add ginger and stir well.

8 Remove pork from fridge and cut into 3cm cubes. Season cornflour well and place beaten egg in a separate bowl. Fill a deep-fryer one-third full with oil and heat to 180°C (see cooking notes, page 264). Dust half the pork with cornflour, dip in egg, dust again with cornflour and deep-fry for 4 minutes or until golden. Remove with a slotted spoon, drain on paper towel and repeat with remaining pork. Serve with the apple slaw, crackling, rice cakes and dressing.

RISE & SHINE!

The last 12 aprons are handed out and the Top 24 arrive in the deserted MasterChef kitchen. The clock is ticking ominously on the wall, but will anyone notice? Surfer Hayden makes the 'dish that changed his life' and pins an immunity pin to his baseball cap. An exhausting bake-off of epic proportions sees the red team go to elimination and it's goodbye to Tom.

FILMING DIARY

Sunday

EPISODE 7 'Half of you will make it; half of you won't.' The last 12 aprons are won.

Monday

EPISODE 8 The first Top 24 challenge: cook the dish that changed your life.

Tuesday

EPISODE 9 Does the surfer dude have what it takes to win immunity?

Wednesday

EPISODE 10 The first team challenge is a gruelling all-nighter in Sonoma bakery.

Thursday

EPISODE 11 The devastated red team faces elimination. Tom and Kumar step up.

Friday

EPISODE 12 The judges teach the master-class dishes that changed their own lives.

Week 2

HALF IN, HALF OUT

Twenty-four contestants fight it out for the last 12 aprons. Bring on the Matt Moran 'what you pick is what you get' taste and invention test. Jay read the recipe the night before but 'somebody flushed the toilet on my memory'.

The Top 24 are announced and Jay nearly lifts Gary off the ground with his hug, but it's goodbye to Alex...

CHANGE YOUR LIFE

Or is it? Alex gets a second chance when RAAF fighter pilot Paul is called away on duty. The Top 24 arrive in the MasterChef kitchen to find the pantry open but nobody home. The huge clock ticks unnoticed on the wall. Some contestants amble down and start cooking, getting a head start in the 'dish that changed your life' challenge. The others then 'all just run to the pantry like a pack of wild animals,' says Chelsea. Kate makes a life-changing

Below: Some of the contestants get a head start in the challenge, others have to race to catch up.

taken away to run Sonoma bakery for the night. Kumar's excited because he loves baking bread, and Rachel's thrilled to be in the red team because she thinks it won every challenge last series.

Five different loaves have to be delivered to top Sydney restaurants at 8am. The blue team starts off with the wrong ciabatta dough but snatch victory by the narrowest of margins.

GOODBYE TO TOM

'We worked so well in the challenge, it just doesn't seem fair,' says Danielle, but the devastated red team has to choose two members to go 'in the round'. Tom, like the captain of the *Titanic*, steps forward, and ciabatta-baking Kumar joins him. 'It's been a hell of a ride,' says gentleman Tom, leaving the kitchen after just one week.

Clockwise from below: The red team tries to catch up on some sleep while contestants await the results of the exhausting Sonoma challenge; Chef Alessandro explains the rules of the immunity challenge to his valiant apprentice: 'Alex, if you lose, I cut your head off.'

'Boom, boom, bake the room!'

George (of course)

coffee cake; Billy cooks a cake that didn't change his life, but uses chocolate, which did. Jay cooks the lamb roast he'd 'miss footy training for' and George is smitten.

HAYDEN'S TAN STARTS TO FADE

Hayden's moules won the challenge so he cooks for the first immunity pin. He's up against Ormeggio's Alessandro Pavoni, or rather his star apprentice, Alex. Hayden gets a recipe for agnolotti bagoss; Alex doesn't. Hayden wins by a point and Alex says he'd like to go surfing with him. Gary points out that Hayden's been in the kitchen so long his surfy tan is fading.

A NIGHT IN THE BAKERY

It's 11.33pm. 'I've had about one hour's sleep,' says Sun. 'Rise and shine, sweethearts,' shouts George gleefully as the contestants are shuffled into cars and

Serves **4**
Preparation **30 minutes**
Cooking **55 minutes**

Andrew's
CARROT & GINGER POTSTICKERS
WITH CRISPY CHICKEN & BROTH

There were 24 contestants and only 12 places left, so nerves were frayed during this invention test. There were a few dumplings on the tasting bench, but Andrew's potstickers in broth won him a white apron. 'This does everything a great MasterChef dish should do,' said Matt Preston in admiration.

2 chicken thighs, bone in, skin on
SOY MARINADE
60ml (¼ cup) soy sauce
2 cloves garlic, sliced
2cm piece ginger, sliced
1 star anise
BROTH
1 chicken carcass
2 chicken wings

500ml (2 cups) duck or chicken
   stock
3 star anise
2cm piece ginger, sliced
2 eschalots, sliced
200g shiitake mushrooms
POTSTICKER DUMPLINGS
2 tbs olive oil
1 carrot, peeled and sliced

4 coriander roots, scraped
2cm piece ginger, julienned
¼ cup coriander leaves
¼ cup celery leaves
1 tbs soy sauce
1 egg yolk
12 gow gee wrappers
Micro coriander leaves, to serve

1 **To make soy marinade,** mix together all ingredients in a bowl. Debone chicken thighs, keeping bones for stock. Toss thighs in marinade and leave in fridge until required.

2 **To make broth,** preheat oven to 200°C. Place chicken carcass, wings and thigh bones in a lightly greased roasting pan and roast for 30 minutes or until deep golden. Transfer bones to a large saucepan and add duck stock, star anise, ginger, eschalots and 150ml water. Bring to the boil, reduce heat to low and simmer, uncovered, for 25 minutes or until reduced by one-third. Strain, keeping the eschalots.

3 **To make dumplings,** heat oil in a large frying pan. Add carrot, coriander root, ginger and 2 tbs water and cook over medium heat for 5 minutes or until tender. Cool. Process coriander and celery leaves, soy sauce and yolk in a food processor with carrot mixture until finely chopped.

4 Place 1 level teaspoon of dumpling filling in the centre of a gow gee wrapper. Brush edges with water. Fold wrapper over into a half-moon shape and press edges together gently to seal. Repeat with remaining dumpling filling and wrappers.

5 Remove chicken thighs from the marinade and pat dry with paper towel. Heat a large non-stick frying pan over high heat, add chicken thighs and cook, skin-side-down, for 5 minutes, then turn over and cook for 3 minutes or until cooked through. Slice to serve.

6 Cook the sliced eschalot in the same pan for 3 minutes or until crisp and golden. Drain on paper towel and set aside.

7 Cook dumplings in boiling water for 3 minutes or until wrappers are softened and cooked through. Place 500ml (2 cups) of the broth in a small saucepan and bring to a simmer. Add shiitake mushrooms and cook for 2 minutes or until tender.

8 Arrange dumplings and crispy chicken in bowls. Ladle in broth and mushrooms and garnish with fried eschalots and micro coriander.

Serves **4**
Preparation **40 minutes**
Cooking **45 minutes**

Hayden's
MOULES FRITES

'I knew what I was going to cook straightaway,' said Hayden of the 'dish that changed his life'. He poached the mussels in their own juices and a little white wine and made chips that were crunchy and soft. 'It's no fuss but it's beautiful. It's one of those dishes the four of us could share... with a beer,' he said, bringing out a bottle for the judges.

POMMES FRITES
8 russet potatoes, scrubbed
Vegetable oil, to deep-fry
2 tbs herbes de Provence,* ground
2 tsp sea salt

MOULES MARINIERES
1 tbs olive oil
40g butter
2 large cloves garlic, finely chopped
2 large eschalots, finely diced
1 bay leaf

1 tbs chopped thyme
2 spring onions, thinly sliced
1kg black mussels, scrubbed, bearded
250ml (1 cup) dry white wine
60ml (¼ cup) thick cream

1 To make pommes frites, cut potatoes into chunky chips approximately 8 x 1.5 x 1.5cm.
2 Put chips in a saucepan of salted water and bring to boil over high heat. Reduce heat to low and simmer for 6 minutes or until par-boiled. Drain well and pat dry with paper towel. Put on an oven tray and refrigerate for about 30 minutes.
3 Fill a deep-fryer or large saucepan one-third full with vegetable oil and heat to 170°C (see cooking notes, page 264). Working in 3 batches, fry chips for 5 minutes or until golden and cooked through. Drain on paper towel and set aside. Increase oil temperature to 190°C.
4 For the mussels, heat a large frying pan or wok over medium heat. Add olive oil and half the butter. Swirl to combine then add garlic, eschalots, bay leaf, thyme and spring onions. Cook for 3 minutes or until soft and translucent, stirring often to avoid browning.
5 Add mussels, cover pan and cook for 4 minutes, shaking the pan occasionally. Add wine, cover and cook for a further 2 minutes, shaking pan to coat mussels and deglaze pan. Check to see if mussels are open: if most have not opened, replace lid and cook for a further minute or two.
6 When all mussels have opened, use a slotted spoon to transfer to a large bowl. Discard any unopened mussels. Cover bowl and keep warm.
7 Strain liquid through a fine sieve into a small saucepan and bring to the boil over high heat. Cook for 5 minutes or until reduced by one-third. Add cream and remaining butter and whisk until melted and smooth. Season with salt and pepper to taste and pour into a serving jug.
8 Deep-fry chips again in 3 batches for 2 minutes or until crisp. Drain well and season with herbes de Provence and salt. Serve with mussels and sauce.

TIP **Herbes de Provence** is a dried herb mixture of thyme, marjoram, parsley, tarragon, lavender, celery seeds and bay leaves. Available from specialist food shops and good delis.

'Crispy chips, perfectly cooked mussels, delicious tasty sauce... what more can we say?' George

Kate's
RETRO COFFEE CAKE
WITH STICKY APPLES

'No coffee cake is going to win MasterChef,' said Gary, but ended up eating his words along with the cake. 'You need to take it away now because I want more.' When Kate was a little girl she was bored in the summer holidays and her mum gave her a day in the kitchen. This is what she made on the day she fell in love with cooking.

COFFEE CAKE
250g unsalted butter, softened
220g (1 cup) caster sugar
1 tsp vanilla bean paste
4 eggs
300g (2 cups) self-raising flour
160ml (2/3 cup) milk, at room
   temperature
80ml (1/3 cup) espresso, cooled

20g (1/4 cup) flaked almonds,
   roasted
STICKY APPLES
220g (1 cup) caster sugar
1 tsp ground cinnamon
1 star anise
1 large granny smith apple,
   peeled, cored, thickly sliced
2 tbs Kahlua or Tia Maria

COFFEE BUTTERCREAM
250g unsalted butter, softened
320g (2 cups) icing sugar, sifted
60ml (1/4 cup) espresso, cooled
1 tbs Kahlua or Tia Maria

1 To make coffee cake, preheat oven to 180°C. Grease a 20 x 30cm slice pan and line with baking paper so that paper overhangs the long sides. Using an electric mixer, beat butter, sugar and vanilla until pale and fluffy. Add eggs, one at a time, beating well after each addition. Sift in flour, pour in milk and coffee and gently fold together until combined and smooth (don't worry if the mixture appears curdled).

2 Pour into the pan, smooth the surface and bake for 30 minutes, or until cake springs back to a gentle touch. Cool in pan for 5 minutes, then turn onto a wire rack to cool completely.

3 To make sticky apples, stir sugar, cinnamon, star anise and 250ml (1 cup) water in a saucepan over low heat without boiling until sugar has dissolved. Add apple, increase heat to high and bring to the boil. Reduce heat to medium and simmer for 8 minutes or until apples are tender. Lift out apples with a slotted spoon. Cook syrup for 10 minutes or until reduced by half. Return apples to syrup and add liqueur.

4 To make coffee buttercream, use an electric mixer to beat butter until pale. Gradually add icing sugar, then coffee and liqueur and beat until light and fluffy.

5 To serve 'MasterChef-style', as Kate did, use a biscuit cutter to cut six 8cm rounds from the cake. Cut each round in half horizontally, spread buttercream over the top of each round and layer three together to make a small triple-layered cake. Spread remaining buttercream over sides of cakes with a palette knife. Alternatively, slice whole cake in half horizontally and fill with buttercream, then spread remaining buttercream over top of cake. Scatter cake with almonds and serve with sticky apples and syrup.

'I tried to "MasterChef" the cake up a bit!' Kate

Billy's
FLOURLESS CHOCOLATE CAKE

FLOURLESS CHOCOLATE CAKE	PASTRY BASE	POMEGRANATE AND SOUR
125g unsalted butter, chopped	150g (1 cup) plain flour	CHERRY SAUCE
220g (1 cup) caster sugar	80g (½ cup) icing sugar	2 tbs pomegranate molasses
300g dark chocolate (70%	70g cold unsalted butter,	2 tbs icing sugar
cocoa solids), chopped	chopped	TO SERVE
125ml (½ cup) thickened cream	1 egg, lightly beaten	1 tbs orange zest
5 eggs, lightly beaten	GRAND MARNIER CREAM	Dark (Dutch) cocoa
200g (1 cup) drained sour	300ml crème fraîche	Pomegranate seeds
morello cherries, patted dry	1 tbs icing sugar	
(keep 125ml/½ cup of liquid)	60ml (¼ cup) Grand Marnier	
25g (¼ cup) dark (Dutch) cocoa	1 tbs orange zest	

1 To make chocolate cake, preheat oven to 180°C. Grease a 20 x 30cm slice pan and line with baking paper, so that paper overhangs the long sides. Melt butter and sugar in a saucepan over low–medium heat, stirring occasionally. Remove from heat and cool.

2 Fill a small saucepan one-third full with water and bring to a gentle simmer. Place chocolate and cream in a small heatproof bowl, place over pan (don't let the bowl touch the water) and stir until melted and smooth. Pour chocolate mixture into butter mixture and stir until smooth. Add eggs and mix together.

3 Pour mixture into pan and scatter cherries on top. Bake for 20 minutes or until set on the sides but still a bit wobbly in the centre. Remove from oven, cool, then refrigerate until cold.

4 To make pastry base, line an oven tray with baking paper. Process flour, icing sugar, butter and a pinch of salt in a food processor until mixture resembles crumbs. Add egg and process until mixture just comes together. Shape into a rectangle, wrap in plastic and refrigerate for 15 minutes to rest.

5 Roll out pastry on a sheet of baking paper to 21 x 31cm. Transfer to an oven tray and bake for 12 minutes or until golden; cool.

6 For Grand Marnier cream, whisk crème fraîche and icing sugar in a bowl until soft peaks form. Add Grand Marnier and whisk until combined. Fold in orange zest and refrigerate until required.

7 For pomegranate and sour cherry sauce, place pomegranate molasses, icing sugar and the 125ml reserved sour cherry liquid in a small saucepan and bring to the boil over medium–high heat. Cook for 5 minutes or until reduced by half. Remove from heat and leave to cool.

8 Dust a board with cocoa powder and turn out cake. Remove baking paper. Flip pastry base onto cake and remove baking paper. Lay a second chopping board on top of pastry and invert the whole thing so the cake is on top of the pastry. Trim any excess pastry. Cut in half lengthwise, then cut each half into 6 slices.

9 Serve slices of cake with Grand Marnier cream. Drizzle with pomegranate and sour cherry sauce. Sprinkle with orange zest, a dusting of cocoa powder and pomegranate seeds to serve.

Chef Alessandro Pavoni's
AGNOLOTTI BAGOSS WITH BASIL SAUCE

ROASTED TOMATOES
250g rock salt
10 baby roma tomatoes, halved
   lengthwise
Extra virgin olive oil, to drizzle
FILLING
500ml (2 cups) pouring cream
4g gold-strength gelatine
   leaves
150g bagoss* cheese, grated

PASTA
210g '00' pasta flour, sifted
90g fine semolina
2 eggs
4 egg yolks
80g (½ cup) fine semolina, extra,
   to dust
BASIL SAUCE
1 cup basil leaves
50g baby spinach

80ml (⅓ cup) extra virgin olive
   oil
20g grated parmesan
ANCHOVY CRUMBS
5 anchovies, finely chopped
10g butter
20g coarse breadcrumbs from
   day-old bread
Finely grated parmesan and olive
   oil, to serve

1 **To roast tomatoes,** preheat oven to 120°C. Spread the salt in a shallow oven tray. Place
   tomatoes, cut-side-up, on salt and drizzle with oil. Roast for 1 hour or until semi-dried.
2 **To make filling,** pour cream into a deep frying pan and place over high heat. Bring to the boil,
   reduce heat to medium and simmer, stirring regularly, for 8 minutes or until cream has reduced
   to one-third (do not allow to boil over).
3 Meanwhile, soften gelatine in cold water for 3 minutes, then squeeze out excess water. Remove
   cream from heat, add gelatine and stir until dissolved. Pour into a metal bowl and stir in cheese.
   Place over a bowl of ice and stir until cooled completely. Mixture will be quite firm but pliable.
   Spoon into a piping bag and refrigerate until 5 minutes before needed.
4 **For pasta,** pulse flour, semolina, eggs and yolks in processor until mixture forms a ball. Knead
   on floured bench for 5 minutes until smooth and elastic. Wrap in plastic and chill for 15 minutes.
5 **Meanwhile, to make basil sauce,** half-fill a small saucepan with water and bring to the boil.
   Blanch basil and spinach for 10 seconds, then refresh in iced water. Squeeze out excess water.
   Blend with the oil, parmesan and 100ml cold water until smooth.
6 **For anchovy crumbs,** dry-fry anchovies in a small frying pan for 1 minute, stirring to break
   down further. Add butter and breadcrumbs and cook, stirring, for 2 minutes until golden.
7 Divide pasta dough into 4 equal portions. Using a rolling pin, flatten 1 portion to 3mm thick and
   about 12cm wide. Set pasta machine at widest setting, then feed the dough through, narrowing
   settings one notch at a time until you reach the thinnest setting. Repeat with remaining dough.
8 Lightly dust a work surface with semolina. Lay pasta sheet on work surface. Pipe 5 small piles
   of filling at 10cm intervals along the centre of each sheet. Fold pasta in half lengthwise and
   press firmly around the filling, pressing out air between the filling and pasta. Cut out agnolotti
   with a crimping tool, about 7mm from the filling. Toss agnolotti gently in semolina to dust.
9 Cook agnolotti in a large saucepan of boiling salted water until it floats to the surface; drain.
   Place a few agnolotti and tomato halves on plates, dot with basil sauce and sprinkle with
   anchovy crumbs, grated parmesan and a few drops of olive oil.

TIP **Bagoss** is an Italian cheese. You can find it in specialist cheese shops. Use pecorino if you can't find bagoss.

Chef Alessandro took both Hayden and apprentice Alex under his wing in the first immunity challenge.

Makes **about 40 pieces**
Preparation **30 minutes**
Cooking **45 minutes**

Kumar's
BAKLAVA

Chef Abla Amad, from Abla's Lebanese restaurant in Carlton, brought in her favourite ingredient – pistachios – for Tom and Kumar to cook with in the first elimination challenge. She wanted them to cook baklawa for her (the Lebanese dish that the Greeks call 'baklava'), without using a recipe. Neither man had ever made one, but both had 'eaten quite a few'.

250g unsalted butter, melted
375g filo pastry
260g (2 cups) finely ground cashews

70g (¹/2 cup) coarsely ground pistachios

SUGAR SYRUP
330g (1¹/2 cups) caster sugar
10 whole cloves

1 Preheat oven to 220°C. Brush a 25 x 35cm (5cm deep) baking pan with melted butter. Trim the pastry sheets to fit the pan. Layer half the pastry into the pan, brushing every second sheet with melted butter.

2 Spread the cashews and half the pistachios evenly over the pastry. Cover with the remaining filo, brushing every second sheet with butter. Do not butter the top sheet yet.

3 Using a very sharp knife, cut the baklava into small diamonds, making sure you cut right down to the pan. Brush the remaining butter over the top.

4 Bake for 10 minutes. Reduce the oven to 180°C and bake for another 35 minutes or until golden. Remove from the oven.

5 To make sugar syrup, put sugar, cloves and 500ml (2 cups) water in a saucepan. Place over high heat and gently move the pan around but do not stir – swirl the pan until the sugar has dissolved. Bring to the boil, reduce heat and simmer for 10 minutes or until thick and syrupy.*

6 Pour hot syrup over hot pastry, sprinkle with remaining pistachios and leave to cool in the pan.

TIP Abla gave Tom and Kumar a great tip on the show: if you make your sugar syrup in advance, squeeze in a little lemon juice to prevent sugar crystals forming.

'The syrup is to be like honey... soft honey.' Abla

BATTLE OF THE SEXES

There's a rabbit in the mystery box and every ingredient must be used, leaving some contestants awaiting 'divine inspiration'. Jay cooks a cracker dish and goes for immunity, while Billy takes a risk by stamping his own 'personality' on a bombe Alaska. The girls set the world on fire during a night out at the pub and we say goodbye to Alex and Seamus.

FILMING DIARY

Sunday

EPISODE 13 Use all 11 ingredients from the rabbit mystery box, or you're out.

Monday

EPISODE 14 It's an elimination with a bang – or rather, a bombe.

Tuesday

EPISODE 15 Jay puts on chef's whites to cook steak and kidney pie for immunity.

Wednesday

EPISODE 16 It's a lovely relaxing night at the pub – MasterChef style.

Thursday

EPISODE 17 The boys have just 10 minutes to cook their way to safety.

Friday

EPISODE 18 George cooks rabbit and Gary makes shepherd's pie in masterclass.

Week 3

BOX OF BUNNIES

'If you want to be the last cook standing, it's time to break away from the pack,' says Gary. The mystery box is opened, and there's a rabbit. 'What am I going to do with a rabbit?' asks Craig. 'I don't even like rabbit.' And it gets worse: they have to cook a rabbit dish using every single ingredient in the box – including mustard fruit. Dani's never cooked with them before but she's going to use her intuition. 'Great,' says George, dryly. 'Thank goodness you're not flying a plane today.'

WHO'S GOING TO BOMBE?

It's pressure test time for the bottom three bunny-boilers: Alex (steamed rabbit mousse that gave Gary a 'horrible sensation'), Ellie (raw rabbit with 'suede') and Billy (rabbit belly in plastic wrap). They're presented with a bombe Alaska that sends Alex home for good.

Below: It's time to put out the fires and get the food on the plate. Adam damps down the flames and Alex strives to rise above the competition with an ambitious rabbit mousse.

service at the Mean Fiddler pub. The blue team's grill catches fire. 'Brilliant,' says Craig, 'I'm going to die in the Mean Fiddler.' George's lips pucker in horror at the girls' jus: 'There's something in there I've never tasted before.' It's the gravy powder Rachel's decided to add.

It's service time and everything's falling apart... the boys' steaks are sent back almost as fast as Mat can cook them. Jay's fantastic pork belly and Seamus and Kumar's dessert almost save the day but, despite their fire and gravy disgrace, the girls win on diner votes.

The boys go into an elimination challenge, cooking against each other in three super-quick rounds that produce some of the best dishes so far. Sadly, someone always has to go home, and today it's Seamus's turn to say goodbye.

Below: They're a tough crowd to please at the Mean Fiddler. The boys' team is almost saved by Kumar and Seamus's meringue-mess dessert... but not quite.

It's short-order disorder in the Mean Fiddler pub as George uncovers Gravy-gate.

A TOUGH CHALLENGE FOR JAY

Jay was deservedly 'proud as punch' of the restaurant-quality rabbit dish that won him Sunday's challenge. Now he gets to cook steak and kidney pie against Colin Fassnidge from Sydney's Four in Hand. 'The last time I made pastry I was a student, so I was hungover,' admits Colin. He makes suet pastry from scratch, while Jay gets his filling stuck in the pressure cooker. The chef wins convincingly but Jay's had a great time. 'Colin, I wouldn't have got a dish up without you,' says Jay. 'Great. You owe me a car,' says Colin.

THE BATTLE OF THE SEXES

Surely it's time for a night out at the pub? The girls are the blue team, the boys are the red, and they're taking over dinner

Serves **4 as a starter**
Preparation **45 minutes**
Cooking **1 hour 15 minutes**

Cleo's
LOIN OF RABBIT STUFFED
WITH OLIVES & CARAMELISED LEEK

Jay, Cleo and Craig cooked the best three dishes in the rabbit mystery box challenge. Cleo used to watch her mother cook with rabbit so she was full of ideas. The flavours of this dish worked so beautifully together that the judges were thrilled.

ROAST SWEDE
1 swede, peeled, diced
1 tbs extra virgin olive oil
1 tsp lemon thyme leaves
CARROT PUREE
40g butter
1/2 leek, sliced
2 carrots, peeled and diced
50ml white wine

MUSTARD FRUIT SYRUP
1/2 leek, thinly sliced
150ml white wine
1 clove garlic, crushed
1 sprig lemon thyme
50ml mustard fruit syrup[*]
1 tbs lemon juice or to taste
RABBIT
20g butter

1/2 leek, finely chopped
1/2 clove garlic, crushed
5 Sicilian olives, finely chopped
6 thin slices pancetta
2 rabbit loins, trimmed (ask your
    butcher to do this)
1 tbs olive oil
Lemon thyme and thinly sliced
    pear mustard fruits,[*] to serve

1 For the roast swede, preheat oven to 180°C and line an oven tray with baking paper. Cook swede in a saucepan of boiling water for 10 minutes or until tender; drain. Place on tray, toss in oil, sprinkle with thyme and roast for 15 minutes or until golden. Keep warm.

2 To make carrot purée, melt half the butter in a saucepan and cook leek for 5 minutes over medium heat until tender. Add carrots and cook for 3 minutes, then add wine and 250ml (1 cup) water and cook for 20 minutes or until carrot is tender. Drain and purée with remaining butter, then press through a sieve. Season to taste and keep warm.

3 To make mustard fruit syrup, put leek, wine, garlic and thyme in a small saucepan. Bring to the boil over medium heat. Reduce the heat slightly and simmer for 10 minutes or until thickened and reduced; strain. Add mustard fruit syrup and cook for a further 3 minutes. Add lemon juice to taste.

4 For rabbit, heat butter in a small frying pan over medium heat and cook leek and garlic for 5 minutes or until soft. Add olives and mix well. Arrange pancetta, overlapping slightly, on a piece of plastic wrap. Place rabbit loin on top. Slice a pocket in the rabbit loin and fill with olive mixture. Roll tightly in plastic wrap and refrigerate for 15 minutes.

5 Bring a large deep frying pan half-filled with water to a simmer. Poach the plastic-wrapped rabbit for 5 minutes. Unwrap, place on an oven tray and drizzle with olive oil. Roast at 180°C for 5 minutes or until browned. Rest for 5 minutes, then cut into 3cm slices.

6 To serve, smear a little carrot purée across the serving plate. Place two slices of rabbit onto the plate, arrange roasted swedes around and drizzle with syrup. Garnish with lemon thyme leaves and sliced pear mustard fruits.

TIP **Pear mustard fruits** are candied pears preserved in a mustard-flavoured syrup. Available from good delis.

'This makes me so happy... it's an absolutely delicious dish.' George

Serves **8–10**
Preparation **1 hour 20 minutes + 6 hours freezing**
Cooking **25 minutes**

Elimination
COCONUT CHERRY BOMBE ALASKA

330g (1¹/₂ cups) caster sugar
4 egg whites
COCONUT ICE-CREAM
80ml (¹/₃ cup) thickened cream
250ml (1 cup) milk
1¹/₂ tbs liquid glucose
25g (¹/₃ cup) shredded coconut,
   toasted

6 egg yolks
75g (¹/₃ cup) caster sugar
150ml coconut cream
CHERRY SORBET
110g (¹/₂ cup) caster sugar
1 lemon, juiced, zest cut
   into strips
280g frozen pitted cherries

SPONGE
10 egg yolks
220g (1 cup) caster sugar
6 egg whites
75g (¹/₂ cup) plain flour, sifted
40g cornflour, sifted
80g unsalted butter, melted and
   cooled

1 For ice-cream, put cream, milk, glucose and coconut in a saucepan and bring almost to the boil. Meanwhile, whisk together egg yolks and sugar, then whisk in coconut cream. Gradually combine milk mixture with yolk mixture, whisking gently. Transfer to a clean saucepan over medium heat and stir without boiling until thick enough to coat the back of a wooden spoon.

2 Strain through a fine sieve into a bowl. Put bowl in a sink of ice and cool, stirring occasionally, for 15 minutes. Cover with plastic and put in fridge for 45 minutes. Churn in an ice-cream machine until frozen. Put in an airtight container and freeze for 45 minutes or until very firm.

3 To make sorbet, stir sugar, zest and 125ml (¹/₂ cup) water in a saucepan over medium heat until sugar dissolves. Cover pan, bring to the boil and cook for 5 minutes. Add cherries, reduce heat and simmer for 3 minutes until softened. Discard zest, pour into a bowl and cool for 15 minutes.

4 Mix in a food processor until smooth. Strain through a fine sieve, then stir in lemon juice. Chill for 45 minutes, then churn in an ice-cream machine for 35 minutes or until frozen.

5 To make sponge, preheat oven to 160°C. Grease a 26 x 36cm oven tray and an 18cm springform pan with oil and line with paper. With electric mixer, whisk egg yolks with half the sugar until thick and pale. Whisk egg whites and a pinch of salt to soft peaks. Add remaining sugar, 2 tbs at a time, whisking until stiff peaks form. Fold one-third of the egg white into the yolk mixture with a metal spoon. Gently fold in remaining egg white. Fold in flours, then the butter. Spoon 2 cups of the batter into the pan and spread remainder in the tray. Bake for 15 minutes or until golden and springy to touch. Cool, then turn out both sponges onto a wire rack.

6 To assemble, lightly grease a 2.25L pudding basin and line base with baking paper. Cut sponge rectangle in half widthways, then trim each half into an 18 x 26cm rectangle. Cut each rectangle into four 4.5 x 26cm rectangles, then cut each in half on the diagonal to make 16 long triangles.

7 Line the pudding basin snugly with sponge triangles, points downwards, leaving no gaps. Trim sponge layer 2cm from the top of the basin. Freeze for 10 minutes to firm. Spread a 2cm-thick layer of ice-cream over sponge. Spoon sorbet into the centre. Top with the sponge round; it should sit inside the pudding basin. Cover with plastic wrap and freeze for 4 hours or until firm.

8 Stir sugar and 60ml (¹/₄ cup) water in a saucepan over low–medium heat until dissolved. Brush down side of pan with a wet brush to stop crystals forming. Increase heat to medium and cook without stirring for 4 minutes or until 115°C. Whisk egg whites and a pinch of salt to soft peaks. Mix in syrup in a slow stream, then whisk at high speed for 10 minutes until stiff and glossy.

9 Turn out pudding (to remove basin, wipe with a hot tea towel). Quickly spoon meringue over bombe, then spread and swirl. Caramelise evenly with a blowtorch and serve immediately.

Dani's
SALT & PEPPER PRAWNS WITH LIME AIOLI

The prawns were 'dish of the day' and won most votes in the Mean Fiddler challenge; Dani cooked them up as the 'snack' part of the girls' menu. 'These are juicy, salty, peppery – just what you like to eat with a beer,' said Matt Preston. The Mean Fiddler diners agreed.

Vegetable oil, to deep-fry
20 green tiger prawns, peeled
    with tails intact, cleaned
2 egg whites, lightly beaten
Lime wedges, to serve
LIME AIOLI
3 egg yolks

250ml (1 cup) vegetable oil
2 cloves garlic, finely chopped
1 lime, juiced
SEASONING
75g (½ cup) cornflour
1 tsp ground white pepper
1 tbs sea salt

1 tsp Chinese five-spice
½ tsp ground coriander
2 tsp chilli powder
2 tsp ground Szechuan pepper*

1 **To make lime aïoli,** whisk egg yolks until pale. Whisking continuously, add oil, drop by drop at first, then in a thin steady stream until thick and emulsified. Whisk in garlic and lime juice and season with salt and pepper to taste.
2 **To make the seasoning,** combine all the ingredients in a bowl.
3 Fill a deep-fryer or large saucepan one-third full with vegetable oil and heat over medium heat to 190°C (see cooking notes, page 264). Working in small batches, dip prawns in egg white, then in seasoning mix, ensuring prawns are thickly coated. Gently drop prawns into the oil and fry for 2 minutes or until golden and cooked through. Drain on paper towel and serve with lime aïoli and lime wedges.

TIP **Szechuan pepper** is available from selected supermarkets and Asian grocers.

Serves **4**
Preparation **30 minutes**
Cooking **25 minutes**

Kate's
AUSSIE BEEF BURGERS WITH CHEESE & CARAMELISED ONIONS

Kate's caramelised onions on this burger were an upmarket version of barbecue sauce. They were certainly a big hit with the judging panel. 'What more do you want? That is a ripper burger,' said George. 'The girls have absolutely creamed the guys on this one,' agreed Gary.

CARAMELISED ONIONS
10g butter
2 tsp olive oil
2 onions, thinly sliced
1 tbs red wine vinegar
BEEF PATTIES
500g Wagyu beef mince*
1/2 onion, very finely chopped
1 tbs Dijon mustard

1 egg, lightly beaten
35g (1/2 cup) fresh white
 breadcrumbs
MAYONNAISE
2 egg yolks
2 tsp white vinegar
1 tsp Dijon mustard
200ml grape seed oil
1/2 lemon, juiced

TO SERVE
4 slices cheddar
BBQ sauce
4 hamburger buns, split, toasted
4 iceberg lettuce leaves, trimmed
2 tomatoes, thinly sliced
Thick-cut fries

1 **To make caramelised onions,** heat butter and oil in a frying pan over medium heat until butter has melted. Add onions and cook, stirring occasionally, for 15 minutes or until onions are caramelised. Stir in vinegar and season with salt and pepper.
2 **To make beef patties,** mix mince, onion, mustard, egg and breadcrumbs together and season with salt and pepper. Divide into 4 portions, shape into balls and refrigerate until required.
3 **To make mayonnaise,** whisk together egg yolks, vinegar and mustard in a bowl until thick and pale. Whisking constantly, add oil, drop by drop at first, then in a thin steady stream until thick and emulsified. Season with lemon juice and salt to taste.
4 Flatten the beef patties to just slightly larger than the buns (the patties will shrink slightly during cooking). Preheat a barbecue flat plate or large heavy-based frying pan to medium–high and lightly oil. Cook the patties for 3 minutes on each side for medium–rare, or to your liking. Top with a slice of cheese and a spoonful of caramelised onion.
5 Drizzle BBQ sauce onto the bun bases and top with lettuce leaves, tomato slices, patties, mayonnaise and bun tops. Serve with fries.

TIP **Wagyu beef** is extremely tender meat from Wagyu cattle and is marbled with fat. It is also very expensive, so if you are cooking this for a weekday family dinner you might prefer to use good-quality beef mince instead.

Serves **4 as a starter**
Preparation **10 minutes**
Cooking **5 minutes**

Jay's
SCALLOP, CHORIZO & FENNEL SALAD

Given just 10 minutes to think, run around the pantry, and cook, Jay managed to come up with this wonderful scallop salad in the 'rapid-fire' elimination challenge. The judges felt it could be taken to even greater heights by a punchy vinaigrette – so Jay's added one here.

2 limes
2 baby fennel, trimmed, fronds
 reserved, thinly sliced
2 tsp Dijon mustard
1/2 tsp sweet paprika
1 tsp caster sugar

125ml (1/2 cup) olive oil
1 granny smith apple, halved,
 cored, thinly sliced
2 eschalots, thinly sliced
1 radicchio, trimmed, torn
40g (1/4 cup) pine nuts, roasted

2 dried chorizo, cut into
 5mm slices
20 scallops, without roe
Crusty bread, to serve

1 Segment the limes, place in a small bowl and set aside. Squeeze the juice from the lime membranes through a sieve into another bowl.
2 To make dressing, roughly chop fennel fronds and add to lime juice in bowl. Add mustard, paprika, sugar and half the oil. Whisk together and season with salt and pepper.
3 Toss sliced fennel with apple, eschalots, radicchio and pine nuts in a large bowl. Add dressing and toss gently.
4 Heat 1 tbs of the remaining oil in a large frying pan over high heat and cook chorizo for 1 minute each side or until golden. Tip chorizo and pan juices into the salad. Return the pan to the heat.
5 Heat remaining oil in pan. Cook scallops for 30 seconds each side or until golden and almost cooked. Add scallops to salad. Toss gently and season with salt and pepper.
6 Scatter the salad with lime segments and serve immediately with crusty bread.

Serves **4 as a starter**
Preparation **20 minutes**
Cooking **10 minutes**

Hayden's SCAMPI WITH CHILLI GARLIC BUTTER & PINEAPPLE SALSA

'This is a beautiful-looking dish,' said Gary of Hayden's 'rapid-fire' dish. Hayden's biggest regret of the series was that he was 'the perennial loser' in team challenges, and so missed out on many great rewards. Instead, week after week, he was sent to team eliminations... but then cooked his way out of them with great dishes like this one.

12 small scampi*
Lemon cheeks, to serve

CHILLI GARLIC BUTTER
125g butter, softened
4 cloves garlic, crushed
1 long red chilli, seeded, finely chopped
1 lemon, zested
2 tbs chives, finely chopped

PINEAPPLE SALSA
400g pineapple,* peeled, cut into 1cm pieces
1 avocado, cut into 1cm pieces
1 long red chilli, seeded, thinly sliced
2 eschalots, finely chopped
1/4 cup coriander leaves
1/4 cup mint leaves
1 lime, zested, juiced
1 1/4 tsp sesame oil

1 **To make chilli garlic butter,** combine butter, garlic, chilli, lemon zest and chives in a small bowl, then season with salt and pepper.
2 **To make pineapple salsa,** place all the ingredients in a large bowl, toss well and season.
3 Preheat a chargrill pan or barbecue to high. Using a sharp knife, slice the scampi in half lengthwise and devein. Melt a quarter of the chilli garlic butter in a small saucepan. Remove the pan from heat and, using a pastry brush, brush the scampi with butter. Chargrill scampi, flesh-side-up, in 2 batches, for 2 minutes or until flesh starts to change colour. Turn over and cook for a further minute or until just cooked.
4 Place scampi on a platter and spoon remaining chilli garlic butter over the top. Serve immediately with pineapple salsa and lemon cheeks.

TIP **You can** use large king prawns instead of the scampi. **When mangoes** are in season, this dish is also good with mango salsa. Substitute 2 mangoes for the pineapple.

'My funniest moments on the show were watching Jay do his impersonations, and any time Ellie had to run anywhere!'

Hayden

Michael's

SALMON TARTARE WITH SOFT-BOILED QUAIL EGGS

This was another winner in the all-boy 'rapid-fire' elimination challenge and saved Michael from having to cook again. Don't forget to put a lemon on your shopping list – Michael made a dramatic last-second dash to the pantry for a lemon to tie the flavours together.

12 quail eggs*	1 tsp baby capers, finely chopped	1 lemon, juiced
400g piece salmon fillet, pin-boned, skinned	1 eschalot, finely chopped	60ml (¼ cup) olive oil
10 cornichons,* finely chopped	1 tsp Dijon mustard	Melba toast,* to serve
	1 tbs finely chopped chives	

1 To soft-boil quail eggs, cook eggs in a saucepan of boiling water for 2½ minutes. Drain and refresh in iced water. Peel eggs and set aside.

2 Using a sharp knife, remove any grey sections from the salmon. Finely chop the salmon and place in a bowl with the cornichons, capers, eschalot, mustard and chives. Stir together and season with salt and pepper.

3 Whisk together lemon juice and oil and season to taste.

4 Spread salmon mixture over melba toasts and drizzle with lemon oil. Cut the quail eggs in half and serve one on top of each toast.

TIP **Quail eggs** are available from selected supermarkets and butchers. You can substitute small hen's eggs, boiled for 6 minutes then refreshed in iced water. **Cornichons** are small pickled cucumbers. They are available from supermarkets and delis. **Melba toast** is very dry, crisp, thinly sliced toast, which you can buy from supermarkets and specialty food shops. To make your own, using a rolling pin, roll sliced white bread to 3mm thick, then cut off the crusts. Cut the bread in half on the diagonal, then place on an oven tray and bake in a 180°C oven for 15 minutes or until light golden and crisp.

SMOKE & SIZZLE

Sun, Peter and Craig find joy with their 'pig in a bag', but smoked octopus sees Chelsea packing her bags. Hayden is persuaded to pull on the Cronulla speedos to boost sales at the nippers sausage sizzle, but, despite their secret weapon, the blue team go to elimination. Dessert-demon Billy crushes the opposition, but Cleo can't help multi-tasking and goes home.

FILMING DIARY

Sunday

EPISODE 19 Pick a team, pick an ingredient and pick a cooking technique.

Monday

EPISODE 20 Chelsea, Ellie and Rachel's smoked octopus leads to elimination.

Tuesday

EPISODE 21 It's three against one as Sun, Peter and Craig cook for elusive immunity.

Wednesday

EPISODE 22 Sausages sizzle on the beach for 500 Cronulla nippers.

Thursday

EPISODE 23 Four basic dessert skills must be mastered to avoid elimination.

Friday

EPISODE 24 Gary cooks a one-pot winter warmer and George wraps up parcels.

Week 4

NOT THE OCTOPUS... PLEASE!

'There's got to be some girls going this week, surely?' ponders Craig, staring pointedly at Chelsea and Ellie, who are still celebrating last week's win. It's time to get into teams and lift the cloche on one core ingredient and a cooking technique.

Nobody wants the octopus or brains. And roasting or pan-frying would be great. Sun, Peter and Craig pick pork (happy cheers) and 'en papillote' (confused glances). 'How often do you see meat cooked in a bag?' asks Matt Preston. Well, you're going to see it today.

Chelsea picks octopus. 'I'm just hoping we get a really good technique,' says Ellie. They pick 'smoke'. 'I just want to fling that octopus out of the door,' says Chelsea.

THE SWEET AND THE SOUR

The smoked octopus puts best friends Rachel, Ellie and Chelsea into an elimination without a recipe. Chelsea is

Below: Sun and Billy are just happy not to have picked octopus in the 'ingredient plus technique' challenge.

clown,' shouts Jay in horror as Hayden canters down the beach in a pair of Cronulla budgie-smugglers. It's the Cronulla sausage sizzle and lifeguard Hayden is the blue team's 'secret weapon' in the challenge to feed 500 nippers sausages and gelato. Hayden gets on the PA to spruik, but Kate answers back and at the end of the day Michael's red team is victorious with most money in the till.

DESSERT SKILLS 101

It sounds so simple: sponge, custard, toffee, ganache – in that order – then put them together to make the best dessert and escape elimination. Billy, the self-styled 'dessert queen', puts up a cracking swiss roll with berry coulis, but Cleo confuses the process and is eliminated.

Clockwise from below: Alana and Rachel take the red team's sausages to the masses; Dani and Billy race onto the beach after a long night making gelato; Hayden agrees to help out the blue team by donning a pair of skimpy sluggos.

'The nippers are out, doing their nipper things!' George

bombarded with advice from the balcony and, although her fried rice triumphs, it's her time to go. Rachel hates the dish but 'If Rachel can make sweet and sour sauce this good, I want to ring her up and order black bean beef and cashew chicken to go with it,' says Matt Preston.

THREE AGAINST ONE

'It's some sort of performance cooking he's doing,' says Peter in amazement as he, Sun and Craig take on Adam D'Sylva in a three-against-one immunity challenge. 'I like those odds,' says Craig, until he sees Adam cook – the kitchen is his stage, he 'loves an audience' and the win is his.

SIZZLING SAUSAGES

'You're kidding! It's not a bloody fashion parade. Get back on the barbecue, you

Serves **4**
Preparation 1½ **hours**
Cooking 2½ **hours**

Craig, Peter & Sun's
PORK EN PAPILLOTE ('PIG IN A BAG')

MASTERSTOCK
125ml (½ cup) light soy sauce
125ml (½ cup) dark soy sauce
125ml (½ cup) rice wine
2 star anise
2 cardamom pods, bruised
PORK BELLY IN BLACK BEAN
500g pork belly
30g (¼ cup) black beans
1 tbs hoisin sauce
1 tbs palm sugar
1 clove garlic, finely chopped

½ tsp finely chopped red chilli
½ red capsicum, cut into julienne
60g rice vermicelli noodles
PORK MEATBALLS
500g pork shoulder, chopped
2 cloves garlic, finely chopped
1 red chilli, diced
2 tbs finely chopped coriander
    root and stems
3cm piece ginger, grated
1 eschalot, finely chopped
1 tbs fish sauce

40g shiitake mushrooms
80ml (⅓ cup) dark soy sauce
1 bunch asparagus, thinly sliced
    diagonally
PORK CRACKLING
1 tsp Chinese five-spice
1 tbs sea salt
Olive oil, to drizzle
SAUCE
2 tbs kecap manis
Zest of 1 lime
2 tsp fish sauce

1 **To make masterstock,** put ingredients in a large saucepan with 1.5L (6 cups) water and bring to the boil. Reduce heat to low and simmer for 10 minutes.

2 **For pork belly in black bean,** cut pork belly into 4cm slices and put in a large saucepan with enough masterstock to cover. Cover, bring to the boil, reduce heat to low and cook for 1½ hours or until tender. Remove pork and cut off skin. Place skin on paper towel and set aside to dry. Cut meat into 5mm slices.

3 Soak black beans in boiling water for 10 minutes; drain. Transfer 250ml (1 cup) masterstock to a small saucepan. Add drained black beans, hoisin sauce, palm sugar, garlic and chilli. Bring to the boil, reduce heat to low and cook for 15 minutes, until reduced and syrupy. Add pork slices and capsicum. Meanwhile, soak noodles in boiling water for 3 minutes or until soft. Drain.

4 Lay out 4 squares of baking paper and arrange a small bed of noodles on each. Spoon pork and capsicum mixture over the noodles. Lift the paper up around the noodles and drizzle with 1 tbs black bean syrup. Gather the paper together and tie with kitchen string.

5 **To make pork meatballs,** preheat oven to 180°C. Put pork shoulder in a food processor with garlic, chilli, coriander, ginger, eschalot, fish sauce, shiitake mushrooms and dark soy sauce. Process in short bursts to mix together. Shape heaped tablespoons of mixture into 12 balls.

6 Lay out 4 squares of baking paper and arrange a small bed of asparagus on each. Top with 3 meatballs, slightly separated. Lift the paper up around the meatballs and drizzle with 1 tbs masterstock. Gather the paper together and tie with kitchen string.

7 Place all paper parcels on a large oven tray and bake for 15 minutes. Remove from oven and leave to rest.

8 **To make pork crackling,** increase oven to 200°C. Combine five-spice, salt and oil and rub over skin. Place skin-side-up on a baking tray and bake for 15 minutes or until crisp. Cut into pieces.

9 **Meanwhile, to make sauce,** bring remaining masterstock to the boil and simmer for 5 minutes until reduced by half. Add kecap manis, lime zest and fish sauce. Simmer for 3 minutes and strain. Serve parcels, wrapped or unwrapped, with sauce and pieces of pork crackling.

Elimination
SWEET & SOUR PORK WITH FRIED RICE

Even though it's Chinese, this sauce uses everyday ingredients from an Aussie pantry and the fried rice is best made with leftover cooked rice from the fridge. The pork shoulder is tenderised before it's deep-fried, just like Rachel did on the show.

PORK

500g pork shoulder, cut into 2cm pieces
1 tsp bicarbonate of soda
2 tbs light soy sauce
135g (3/4 cup) rice flour
75g (1/2 cup) cornflour
1 egg, lightly beaten
310ml (1 1/4 cups) chilled sparkling mineral water
2L vegetable oil, to deep-fry
Plain flour, to dust

SWEET AND SOUR SAUCE

200ml pineapple juice
200ml tomato sauce

200ml white vinegar
200g caster sugar
35g (1/4 cup) cornflour
1 green capsicum, chopped
1 red capsicum, chopped
150g pineapple slices, cut into 2cm pieces
1/2 red onion, chopped

FRIED RICE

2 1/2 tbs vegetable oil
1/2 onion, finely diced
1/4 red onion, finely diced
1/2 carrot, finely diced
1 stalk celery, finely diced
2 cloves garlic, finely chopped

100g lap cheong sausage (or bacon), thinly sliced
100g small peeled cooked prawns
100g chicken thigh fillet, pan-fried and shredded
400g (2 cups) cold cooked long-grain rice
100g frozen peas, thawed
100g bean sprouts
2 tsp soy sauce
4 spring onions, thinly sliced
3 eggs
1 tbs mirin

1 For pork, put pork in a bowl with bicarbonate of soda and soy sauce and toss together. Cover and leave for 15 minutes to tenderise. Sift rice flour and cornflour into a bowl with a pinch of salt and make a well in the centre. Add egg and sparkling water and mix with chopsticks until just combined. Leave to rest for 15 minutes.

2 For sweet and sour sauce, put pineapple juice, tomato sauce, vinegar, sugar and 200ml water in a large saucepan and bring to the boil. Reduce heat to medium. Mix cornflour with 2 tbs water to make a smooth paste. Add to pan and stir well. Cook for 2 minutes or until thickened slightly. Stir in capsicums, pineapple and onion, remove from heat and allow to cool.

3 To make fried rice, heat 2 tbs oil in a large frying pan over medium heat. Cook onions, carrot, celery and garlic for 3 minutes or until soft. Add sausage and cook for 2 minutes or until lightly coloured. Add prawns, chicken and rice and cook, stirring, for 3 minutes or until heated through. Add peas, bean sprouts, soy sauce and half the spring onions. Cook, stirring, for 2 minutes, or until well combined and heated through.

4 Whisk eggs and mirin in a bowl. Heat remaining oil in a frying pan over high heat. Pour in the egg mixture and cook for 2 minutes or until just set. Roll up and thinly slice. Stir into the rice.

5 Fill a deep-fryer or large saucepan one-third full with vegetable oil and heat over medium heat to 180°C (see cooking notes, page 264). Toss pork in plain flour and shake off excess. Working in small batches, dip pork in batter then drop into oil. Fry, turning once, for 2 minutes or until crisp and golden. Drain on paper towel. Serve with fried rice and sweet and sour sauce, garnished with remaining spring onions.

She might not be able to smoke an octopus or make a perfect sweet and sour sauce, but Chelsea was the queen of pasta.

Chef Adam D'Sylva's

BLACK PEPPER OCEAN TROUT WITH GREEN MANGO & SPANNER CRAB SALAD

Peter, Craig and Sun cooked against Adam D'Sylva in their bid for immunity. Adam is part-owner and head chef of Melbourne's Coda restaurant and won *The Age 2008 Good Food Guide's* Young Chef of the Year. Sun described his signature plate as 'three amazingly exquisite little piles' – this sticky, caramelised ocean trout was Peter's part of the challenge.

600g ocean trout fillet
60ml (¼ cup) mirin
Vegetable oil, to shallow-fry
2 eschalots, halved, sliced
2 tbs sesame seeds, lightly
toasted
SAUCE
2 tbs vegetable oil
3 cloves garlic, sliced
4cm piece ginger, julienned

2 long red chillies, seeded,
julienned
2 tbs freshly ground black
peppercorns
100ml chicken stock
1 tbs oyster sauce
2 tbs soy sauce
2 tbs caster sugar
80g cold chopped butter

SALAD
4 kaffir lime leaves, finely
shredded
1 green mango, peeled, julienned
1 long red chilli, halved, seeded,
julienned
½ cup coriander leaves
½ cup Thai basil leaves
120g cooked spanner crab meat
1 lime, juiced

1 Preheat oven to 160°C. Pin-bone trout (see cooking notes, page 264), remove skin and cut into 4 neat pieces. Place in a small bowl with mirin to marinate.

2 Heat oil in a large wok over medium heat and gently fry eschalots for 4 minutes or until golden and crisp. Remove with a slotted spoon and drain on paper towel.

3 Drain oil from wok, leaving 2 tbs remaining. Reheat wok over high heat and sear ocean trout in batches for 1 minute each side or until slightly caramelised. Carefully transfer from the wok to an oven tray. Place in oven for 5 minutes.

4 **To make sauce,** wipe out wok and add oil. Reheat over medium heat. Add garlic, ginger and chilli and fry for 30 seconds until fragrant. Add black pepper, chicken stock, oyster sauce, soy sauce and sugar. Add butter a little at a time, whisking constantly to emulsify. Taste for correct balance of sweet and salty and adjust if necessary. Add trout and coat gently with sauce.

5 **To make salad,** toss together all salad ingredients. Arrange trout on plates and drizzle with sauce. Top with salad and sprinkle with sesame seeds and fried eschalots.

Kate & Ellie's
VANILLA BEAN GELATO

Kate and Ellie were up at 3am to make enough gelato for 500 nippers and their parents. They spent a long night scraping vanilla beans and finely grating lemon zest but it was worth it – the judges loved the true flavours of their gelato. Kate even had enough energy to run onto the beach with her sorbet to divert the crowds of nippers away from Hayden.

375ml (1½ cups) milk
375ml (1½ cups) pouring cream
220g (1 cup) caster sugar

1 vanilla bean, split, seeds
  scraped

1 Put milk, cream, sugar, vanilla bean and seeds in a small pan over low heat and cook, stirring, until sugar dissolves. Pour into a bowl and leave for 10 minutes, stirring often to release heat.
2 Remove vanilla bean. Cover mixture with plastic wrap and refrigerate for 3 hours or until well chilled. Churn in an ice-cream machine until frozen. Transfer to an airtight container and freeze for 4 hours or until firm.

LEMON SORBET

275g (1¼ cups) caster sugar
1 tbs lemon zest
430ml (1¾ cups) lemon juice

1 Put sugar, 500ml (2 cups) water and grated zest in a small saucepan over low heat and cook, stirring, until sugar has dissolved. Bring to the boil and cook for 5 minutes. Stir in the lemon juice and strain into a bowl.
2 Cover with plastic wrap and refrigerate for 3 hours or until well chilled. Churn in an ice-cream machine until frozen. Transfer to an airtight container and freeze for 4 hours or until firm.

Billy's
SWISS ROLL WITH RASPBERRY COULIS

5 egg yolks
110g (1/2 cup) caster sugar
3 egg whites
40g plain flour
20g cornflour
40g unsalted butter, melted,
  cooled
Strawberries and raspberries
CREME ANGLAISE
250ml (1 cup) milk
110g (1/2 cup) caster sugar

1 vanilla bean, split, seeds
  scraped
5 egg yolks
60ml (1/4 cup) thickened cream
PISTACHIO PRALINE
140g (1 cup) pistachios, roasted
220g (1 cup) caster sugar
CHOCOLATE GANACHE
125ml (1/2 cup) thickened cream
175g dark chocolate (70% cocoa
  solids), roughly chopped

RASPBERRY COULIS
150g fresh raspberries
1 tbs caster sugar
MASCARPONE CREAM
250g mascarpone
250ml (1 cup) thickened cream,
  whipped to firm peaks
2 tbs Cointreau
1 tbs lemon zest
1 tbs orange zest
3 strawberries, hulled, quartered

1 **To make sponge,** preheat oven to 160°C. Grease and line a 25 x 38cm (1.5cm deep) oven tray. Using an electric mixer, beat yolks and 50g sugar in a small bowl until thick and pale. In a clean dry bowl beat egg whites with a pinch of salt until soft peaks form. Gradually add remaining sugar to whites and whisk until firm peaks form. Fold a large spoonful of egg white into yolk mixture. Gently fold in remaining egg white with a large metal spoon. Sift flours onto egg mixture and gently fold in until combined. Fold in cooled melted butter.

2 Spoon into oven tray and smooth surface. Bake for 8 minutes or until risen and springy to touch. Turn out onto a clean sheet of baking paper and peel off backing paper.

3 **To make crème anglaise,** combine milk, sugar, vanilla bean and seeds in a saucepan over medium heat. Slowly bring almost to boiling point; remove from heat. Whisk yolks until pale. Slowly pour over the hot milk, whisking to combine. Pour back into a clean pan and stir over low heat for 5 minutes or until thickened; do not boil. Strain into a bowl. Whisk in cream, lay plastic wrap directly onto the surface and refrigerate until required.

4 **To make praline,** spread pistachios over an oven tray lined with baking paper. Stir sugar and 80ml (1/3 cup) water in a small saucepan over low heat without boiling until sugar has dissolved. Increase heat and boil without stirring for 8 minutes or until golden. Pour caramel over pistachios and leave to set. When cool, process in a food processor to coarse crumbs.

5 **To make ganache,** heat cream in a saucepan until almost at boiling point. Put chocolate in a heatproof bowl, pour hot cream over it and leave for 3 minutes until chocolate has softened. Stir until smooth and glossy. Set aside to cool.

6 **To make raspberry coulis,** put raspberries in a small saucepan and stir over medium heat until soft and pulpy. Stir in sugar to dissolve. Strain through a fine sieve and discard solids. Cool.

7 **To make mascarpone cream,** use a spatula to combine mascarpone, whipped cream, Cointreau and zest until smooth and spreadable.

8 Spread sponge with two-thirds of the mascarpone cream and sprinkle with half the praline. Place a line of strawberries along one short edge and roll up the sponge. Coat with mascarpone cream and sprinkle with remaining praline. Cut into slices and serve with a quenelle of ganache, the coulis, berries and crème anglaise.

MINES & VINES

'We've dug a bloomin' big hole, and you've got to dig yourselves out of it,' announce the judges. It's the biggest MasterChef challenge ever – 450 burly miners have to be fed for 24 hours. Tempers are frayed and porridge is burnt. The blue team makes an ecstatic trip to Margaret River, where Kumar cracks a giant egg and Jay cooks for immunity, again.

FILMING DIARY

Sunday

EPISODE 25 The biggest challenge ever — feed 450 miners for 24 hours.

Monday

EPISODE 26 From the mine to the vine – an invention test in Margaret River.

Tuesday

EPISODE 27 Jay's dish wins him a second chance to cook for immunity.

Wednesday

EPISODE 28 It's a 'pantry of pain' – a room stocked with cans and frozen food.

Thursday

EPISODE 29 Kumar and Andrew have just eight steps to fix a massaman curry.

Friday

EPISODE 30 Gary makes fish curry and Matt Moran cooks crab in masterclass.

Week 5

MINING, DINING AND WHINING

It's time for a Western Australian adventure and the biggest challenge ever: feed 450 miners for 24 hours. 'I've been here before,' says Perth-girl Rachel, who has something of a home-ground advantage. 'We're at Sunrise Dam gold mine. My husband worked here for 10 years.' The scenery is overwhelming and so is the challenge – the teams have to organise menus and rosters and win votes from the miners. Jay and Dani are captain and vice-captain of the blues, Danielle and Kate of the reds. Jay's democratic streak costs the blues time, but the vibe among the red team is 'uncertain' says Arena with stunning understatement.

There are disasters: Danielle's burnt cacciatore, Michael's frozen-on-the-plate fish; Jay's deep-fried bacon, Kate's lost porridge... There are squabbles when Sun thinks Danielle has turned off the heat

Below: The enormity of their surroundings matches the enormity of the challenge. 'That crash and rattle is the sound of 450 hungry miners heading to the canteen,' shouts Gary, just in case anyone's sitting around with their feet up.

JAY OUT AT SEA

Jay's amazing 'garden of marron' dish sends him 2km along Busselton Jetty to cook against Cape Lodge chef, Tony Howell. Both men put up stunning dishes and Tony is relieved to win – by 1 point.

SHOCK IN THE PANTRY

'It's all about taking ordinary ingredients, and making them extraordinary.' The contestants rush to the pantry, only to find these ingredients are all canned or frozen. Horror abounds, but Billy proves he can still whip up a world-class dessert that makes George wax lyrical. Kumar and Andrew battle against elimination by fixing a sub-standard massaman curry. Will either of them remember to add the potatoes and peanuts?

Clockwise from below: Who will end up with egg on their face, and who will win the chance for double immunity in the Margaret River invention test? Kumar cracks open his 'Jurassic Park' ostrich egg; Craig is less than thrilled with the canned and frozen contents of his basket.

'The one surprising thing is that no-one's burst into tears.' Sun

under Kumar's curry, only to find Kumar has turned it off himself. ('I'll put a note on it next time,' murmurs Kumar subversively after being scolded.) But there are also triumphs, including Rachel's sticky date pudding, Ellie's apple pie and Kumar's 'seduction' garlic breakfast mushrooms.

The score is so close that 'in politics this would've been a hung parliament'.

BOOM, BOOM, SHAKE THE VINES

The blue team fly to Margaret River's Cape Lodge for a vineyard invention test using fresh local produce: lamb, crab, marron, goat and... an ostrich egg. Jay and Michael battle against each other with a pair of restaurant-quality dishes. Sun's venison dish proves she's no longer an 'ex-vegetarian' struggling with meat; and Kumar practises making nets with an egg that looks big enough to hatch a dinosaur.

Rachel's
STICKY DATE PUDDING

Rachel made the most of her connections at the Sunrise Dam mine, but also won unbiased votes with this sticky date pudding. Both teams were exhausted after feeding 450 miners for 24 hours. The final score came down to just 20 votes and the victorious blues, led by Jay, celebrated with two days in Margaret River, while the reds went back into the kitchen.

PUDDING
340g pitted dried dates
2 tsp bicarbonate of soda
125g unsalted butter, chopped

330g (1½ cups) brown sugar
4 eggs, lightly beaten
1 tsp vanilla extract
335g (2¼ cups) self-raising flour

SAUCE
330g (1½ cups) brown sugar
200ml cream
250g unsalted butter, chopped

1 To make pudding, preheat oven to 150°C. Grease a 26cm springform cake pan and line the base with baking paper. Put dates, bicarbonate of soda and 500ml (2 cups) water in a large saucepan and bring to the boil. Reduce heat to low and cook, stirring, for 3 minutes or until dates are soft and have broken down. Turn off heat and cool slightly.

2 Add butter and stir until melted and combined. Add sugar, eggs and vanilla and stir well. Fold in sifted flour until just combined.

3 Pour into cake pan and bake for 1 hour or until a skewer inserted into the centre of the cake comes out clean. Leave to cool in pan before cutting into wedges to serve.

4 To make sauce, put all ingredients in a saucepan and bring to the boil. Reduce heat and simmer for 3 minutes or until smooth and thickened slightly. Serve with pudding.

'I was so proud to be able to show Ellie a picture of my husband... in a bin.' Rachel

'Last week was really busy, so I'm hoping for a bit of rest now,' said Craig. The judges' letter announced it was time to fly somewhere hot. 'Africa, perhaps?' he mused, optimistically.

Jay's
GARDEN OF MARRON

The prize for winning the mine challenge was a trip to Margaret River. The 'local produce' invention test gave each of the 10 competitors a different ingredient to work with. The marron was Jay's first-choice ingredient and he picked it. 'It's poached, and just done with a few little things that I found in the vegie patch,' he said, modestly, of this winning dish.

2 whole marron
1 tbs olive oil
1 onion, sliced
2 tomatoes, chopped
200ml sauvignon blanc
150g butternut pumpkin, peeled, seeded, chopped

4 baby beetroot, scrubbed, stems trimmed
30g butter, softened, chopped
1 large desiree potato, halved lengthwise
Vegetable oil, to deep-fry
4 zucchini or pumpkin flowers

1½ tbs pouring cream
Baby beetroot leaves and fennel fronds or dill sprigs, to garnish

1 Separate marron heads from tails. Heat olive oil in a frying pan, add onion and tomato and cook for 3 minutes or until just softened. Add marron heads and cook for 8 minutes. Pour in wine, reduce heat to low and simmer for 5 minutes or until liquid has reduced by half. Strain sauce through a fine sieve into a saucepan and set aside until ready to serve.

2 Remove the claws from the marron. Using kitchen string, tie the marron tails to metal spoons to keep them straight during cooking. Cook tails and claws in a large saucepan of simmering salted water for 3 minutes or until just cooked. Remove and plunge into a bowl of iced water.

3 Cook the pumpkin in a large saucepan of boiling salted water for 7 minutes or until tender. Remove with a slotted spoon and drain. Add beetroot to the water and cook for 10 minutes or until tender. Mash pumpkin with butter until smooth and push through a fine sieve.

4 Peel marron tails, cut flesh into 2cm-thick discs and carefully remove claw meat from shells (try to pull out meat in one piece).

5 Using a melon baller, scoop out balls of potato. Fill a deep-fryer or large saucepan one-third full with vegetable oil and heat to 180°C (see cooking notes, page 264). Working in 2 batches, gently drop potato balls into the oil and cook for 4 minutes or until golden and cooked through. Drain on paper towel.

6 Reheat oil to 180°C. Deep-fry zucchini flowers for 2 minutes or until golden and drain on paper towel. Add cream to sauce and gently reheat.

7 **To serve,** drizzle spoonfuls of pumpkin purée over plate. Arrange marron, potatoes, baby beetroot, marron claw and zucchini flowers around each plate. Garnish with baby beetroot leaves and fennel fronds. Finish with a drizzle of sauce.

'You've taken a beautiful product and made it into something even more beautiful.' Gary

Serves **6**
Preparation **20 minutes**
Cooking **25 minutes**

Kumar's
GARDEN VEGETABLES IN AN EGG NET

There was one ingredient nobody wanted in the invention test. 'I'll be happy with anything except the ostrich egg,' said Kumar about 10 seconds before he picked the ostrich egg. Kumar had the run of Clairault Estate's kitchen garden for fresh herbs and vegetables to match with his 'Jurassic Park' egg. He's adapted the recipe here to use chicken eggs!

1 tbs olive oil
25g butter
1 onion, chopped
3 cloves garlic, crushed
1 red capsicum
1 yellow capsicum
1 orange capsicum

1 green capsicum
250g red cherry tomatoes
250g yellow cherry (or teardrop)
   tomatoes
1 tbs chopped parsley
2 tsp chopped thyme
2 tsp chopped rosemary

60ml (¼ cup) white wine
8 eggs, lightly beaten
Olive oil, to fry
Whole chives
Lightly dressed rocket, basil and
   parsley leaves, to serve

1 Heat the olive oil and butter in a large saucepan. Add the onion and cook over medium heat for 5 minutes or until soft. Add the garlic and cook a further 1 minute.

2 Cut the capsicums into wide strips, discarding seeds, core and membrane. Add to the pan and cook for 5 minutes until soft. Add the tomatoes and herbs and cook for 5 minutes until tomatoes are just soft. Add wine to pan and cook for 2 minutes. Season with salt and pepper.

3 The easiest way to make egg nets is to pour the egg into a squeeze bottle. (If you don't have one, just drizzle the egg with a ladle.) Lightly oil a large non-stick frying pan and place over medium heat. Drizzle a little egg from the bottle into the pan in a lacy cobweb pattern. Cook for 1 minute or until set. Carefully lift from pan and repeat to make 6 nets.

4 Lay nets on plates and divide the vegetable mixture among them. Fold egg net over the filling. Serve with chives and salad leaves.

Serves **4**
Preparation **35 minutes**
Cooking **45 minutes**

Chef Tony Howell's
W.A. SEAFOOD STEW

Jay's second immunity challenge took place on 2km-long Busselton Jetty against Cape Lodge chef Tony Howell. Tony had moved from Perth to Margaret River for two weeks to help out in a restaurant and enjoy some surfing and diving… 16 years later he was still living there. The dish he chose for the challenge showcased local seafood in a delicate bisque.

FISH STOCK
1.5 kg whole red emperor, cleaned
1 eschalot, sliced
1 stalk celery, chopped
1 dill stalk, sprigs reserved
4 black peppercorns
BROTH
60ml (1/4 cup) olive oil
8 large green prawns, peeled with tails intact, shells reserved
2 eschalots, finely chopped

1/2 carrot, finely chopped
1/4 fennel bulb, chopped
1 clove garlic, crushed
1/4 tsp fennel seeds
Pinch saffron threads
Pinch cayenne pepper
1 bay leaf
50ml Pernod
2 tbs French brandy
12 large cherry tomatoes, halved
AIOLI
2 egg yolks

1 tsp Dijon mustard
1/2 lemon, juiced
1/4 tsp smoked paprika
1/2 clove garlic, crushed
200ml grape seed oil
SEAFOOD
80ml (1/3 cup) olive oil
2 marron, halved, cleaned
12 mussels, scrubbed, bearded
2 tbs French brandy
12 scallops
4 oysters, shucked

1 To make fish stock, fillet fish; remove and discard pin bones. Discard head. Cut fillets into 8cm triangles and refrigerate until required. Place bones in a saucepan with eschalot, celery, dill stalk, peppercorns and 1.25L (5 cups) water. Bring to a simmer and cook, uncovered, for 15 minutes, skimming surface occasionally. Strain through a fine sieve.

2 To make broth, heat oil in a large saucepan. Add prawn shells. Cook over high heat for 2 minutes or until shells change colour and are well cooked. Reduce heat to medium, add eschalot, carrot, fennel and garlic and cook for 5 minutes or until vegetables are soft.

3 Add fennel seeds, saffron, cayenne and bay leaf and cook for 1 minute. Using a meat mallet, crush mixture to a pulp. Carefully flambé* with Pernod and brandy. Add tomatoes and fish stock. Bring to the boil, reduce heat and simmer for 15 minutes. Strain through a fine sieve lined with paper towel into a clean saucepan. Season with salt and pepper.

4 To make aïoli, place yolks, mustard, lemon juice, paprika and garlic in a bowl. Whisk until pale. Whisking continuously, add oil, drop by drop at first, then in a thin steady stream until thick and emulsified. Season.

5 For seafood, heat olive oil in a large deep frying pan. Add marron and cook for 2 minutes, add prawns and cook for 1 minute, then add fish and cook for 1 minute. Add mussels and flambé with brandy. Add a few ladles of broth, cover and cook for 2 minutes or until mussels have opened. Add scallops and cook, uncovered, for 1 minute. Heat remaining broth.

6 Arrange seafood in bowls and add oysters. Spoon broth from the frying pan over seafood and top up with remaining broth. Serve with aïoli and garnish with dill sprigs.

TIP **To flambé,** add the alcohol and immediately light it with a long match. It will flare and burn out quickly.

Billy's

COCONUT PANNA COTTA & CHOCOLATE MOUSSE WITH GUAVA SORBET

The contestants were shocked by the sight of a pantry stocked only with canned and frozen food. 'It's like a horror story,' murmured Sun, as they gazed around. Billy proved he didn't need fresh ingredients: he produced a dish the judges described as 'like something from a different challenge'. 'This is sex on a plate,' proclaimed George, rather disturbingly.

GUAVA SORBET
2 x 410g cans guava in syrup

COCONUT PANNA COTTA
3 tsp gelatine powder
180ml (3/4 cup) prepared custard
270ml can coconut cream
2 1/2 tbs condensed milk

CHOCOLATE MOUSSE
2 tsp gelatine powder
100ml prepared custard
175g drinking chocolate powder
4 egg whites*
35g (1/3 cup) Milo

RASPBERRY COULIS
135g (1 cup) frozen raspberries, thawed
2 tsp caster sugar

TO SERVE
65g (1/2 cup) raspberries
8 canned lychees

1 **To make guava sorbet,** purée guava and syrup until smooth. Strain and refrigerate for 1 hour or until chilled. Churn in an ice-cream machine until frozen. Transfer to an airtight container and freeze for at least 4 hours, removing from the freezer 10 minutes before serving.

2 **To make coconut panna cotta,** sprinkle gelatine over 2 tbs cold water in a small bowl. Leave for 1 minute to soften, then place bowl in a dish of boiling water and whisk until dissolved.

3 Combine custard, coconut cream and condensed milk in a saucepan and bring to a simmer over medium heat. Cool slightly. Stir in gelatine mixture. Divide among four 125ml (1/2-cup) greased dariole moulds. Refrigerate for 3 hours or until set.

4 **To make chocolate mousse,** sprinkle gelatine over 1 1/2 tbs cold water in a small bowl. Leave for 1 minute to soften. Place bowl in a dish of boiling water and whisk until dissolved.

5 Warm custard in a small saucepan. Whisk in gelatine mixture and stir in drinking chocolate. Transfer to a bowl. Using electric beaters, beat egg whites to stiff peaks. Gently fold one-third of egg whites into mixture until combined. Gently fold in remaining egg whites.

6 Spoon 1 tbs Milo into each of four 180ml (3/4-cup) glasses. Spoon the chocolate mousse into the glasses and refrigerate for 3 hours or until firm.

7 **For raspberry coulis,** put raspberries in a small pan and stir over medium heat until soft and pulpy. Add sugar and stir until dissolved. Strain coulis through a fine sieve and leave to cool.

8 Turn out panna cottas (release seal at edge of mould with a small knife) and serve with coulis, raspberries and lychees. Scoop guava sorbet onto plates and serve immediately.

TIP **For the mousse** in the canned and frozen challenge, Billy used 150ml frozen egg white, thawed.

Elimination
MASSAMAN CURRY

Kumar and Andrew were in 'a world of pain' in the 'canned and frozen' challenge and ended up in elimination – having to fix a massaman curry that lacked many of its major ingredients. Despite the gasps from the balcony, both forgot to add peanuts and potatoes, but Kumar's dish was creamier, with tender meat, and it was time for Andrew to leave the kitchen.

MASSAMAN PASTE
5 dried large red chillies
1/2 tsp cumin seeds
1 tsp coriander seeds
1/2 tsp white peppercorns
1/2 cinnamon quill
140g eschalots, chopped
1 stalk lemongrass, chopped
5 cloves garlic, chopped

2.5cm piece ginger, chopped
1/2 tsp shrimp paste
CURRY
2 tbs vegetable oil
750g chuck steak, trimmed, cut into 3cm pieces
1 large onion, chopped
400ml coconut milk
1 bay leaf

750g desiree potatoes, peeled, cut into 3cm chunks
75g (1/2 cup) unsalted roasted peanuts, chopped
11/2 tbs fish sauce
1 tsp tamarind purée*
1 tsp palm sugar*
Fried shallots* and steamed rice, to serve

1 **To make massaman paste,** chop the chillies and cover with 60ml (1/4 cup) hot water. Soak for 30 minutes. Toast the cumin and coriander seeds, peppercorns and cinnamon in a dry frying pan over medium heat for 3 minutes or until fragrant and slightly coloured. Cool, then use a mortar and pestle to grind to a fine powder.

2 Put chillies and their soaking liquid, ground spices and remaining paste ingredients in a small food processor and process to a smooth paste.

3 **To make curry,** heat half the oil in a large saucepan and cook the beef in 4 batches over medium–high heat for 2 minutes or until well browned, adding more oil as necessary. Set aside. Add the onion to the pan and cook over medium heat for 3 minutes or until soft and golden brown. Add the massaman paste and cook, stirring, for 2 minutes. Return the meat to the pan and stir to coat in the onion mixture.

4 Add the coconut milk, bay leaf and 125ml (1/2 cup) water. Cover and bring to a simmer. Reduce the heat to very low and cook, covered, for 1 hour. Add the potatoes, return to a simmer and cook, partially covered, for a further 30 minutes or until the potatoes are tender.

5 Stir in the peanuts. Season with fish sauce, tamarind purée and palm sugar, to taste. Sprinkle with fried shallots and serve with steamed rice.

TIP Tamarind purée, palm sugar and fried shallots can be found in the Asian food section of supermarkets.

YOUTH VS EXPERIENCE

It's a Spanish invention test with a cruel twist. Jay's superstar week in W.A. is suddenly a distant memory as he struggles in churros chaos, but Danielle's Spanish lamb wins her the chance of immunity. Youth comes second to experience in the Gen X versus Gen Y tag-team challenge and who's that with the judges in the gazebo, waiting to taste the cupcakes?

FILMING DIARY

Sunday

EPISODE 31 Choose a Spanish dish to cook – with someone else's ingredients!

Monday

EPISODE 32 Jay's churros send him to elimination... and it's another dessert.

Tuesday

EPISODE 33 Can Danielle cook Thai fish better than a Danish chef to win immunity?

Wednesday

EPISODE 34 Gen X take on Gen Y in a tag-team challenge with a guest judge.

Thursday

EPISODE 35 A 'one-chicken-many-ways' elimination test sends Arena home.

Friday

EPISODE 36 Kate and Rachel jet off to Malaysia for a Rick Stein masterclass.

Week 6

IT'S A (SPANISH) STITCH-UP

Faces light up at the idea of a Spanish invention test. It's time to choose a pair of core ingredients – lamb and anchovies; sherry and oranges; chorizo and squid – to turn into something fabulous.

Jay, still beaming after week 5, knows exactly what he's going to do with his chorizo and squid. Until Gary and George arrive to swap his carefully chosen basket of ingredients with Arena's box of oranges and dessert goodies. Arena was going to make churros (now she's having a crash course in how to stuff a squid), so Jay gives them a go. The judges call Arena up to taste his offering. She gleefully describes the texture as 'soggy wet sock'.

AN UNEXPECTED EXIT

'To go from the top to the bottom in less than a week is really hard to handle,' says Jay, as his 'stodgeball' churros put him

Below: Peter hopes to bring 'experience and wisdom' to the tag-team challenge: 'Their minds will be going all over the place,' he says of the Gen Y youngsters. Alana, captain of team Gen Y, manages to focus her wandering mind.

'I don't think Gen Y is known for its attention span,' scoffs Sun.

Team captains Alana and Adam weigh everything out, but Adam goes blank and forgets to tell Billy about the devil's food cake. There are other debacles: everyone leaves the Yorkshire puddings to someone else; Arena's cupcakes sink and burn; Ellie leaves a huge chunk of veal in the game pie; and team Gen Y forget to time their beef. 'I'm Gen Y. Why am I doing this?' Mat mutters, as he discovers he's been left to wrangle the elusive Yorkshire puds.

As they walk across the lawn, a glorious figure in pink can be seen with the judges and it's clear whose recipes they've been cooking. 'I never imagined that when I met Nigella Lawson I'd be serving her a grey rib roast,' says Shannon, sadly.

Clockwise from below: Shannon cries when she meets her idol, Nigella; the blue team watch but aren't allowed to call out advice – Sun can't help herself and is given a three-minute time penalty; captain Adam rushes to start the challenge but forgets to pass on word of the devil's food cake.

'I've never felt so starstruck in my life!' Alana

into an elimination with Ellie and Dani. 'I'm going to pull out all stops and stay here,' says Jay. 'Let's hope it's not a dessert.'

It is a dessert... and it's time for a tearful goodbye from the previous week's star.

At the other end of the emotional scale, Danielle cooks Martin Boetz's Thai cod for an immunity pin, but just misses out.

GEN X TAKES ON GEN Y

'Oh, this is so delightful,' says Dani, somewhat naively, when cupcakes are found in the garden. The cupcakes herald a devious tag-team challenge. Each team has to cook the same six dishes, but relay-style. Only the first cook will see the recipes and there are only 60 seconds to gabble top-speed instructions to the next contestant. The teams are announced: under-30s versus over-30s. 'We're definitely going to win,' says Mat. 'We're younger; we've got more of our memory.'

Serves **6**
Preparation **1 hour**
Cooking **2 hours 20 minutes**

Danielle's
LAMB & BEAN SPANISH CASSEROLE WITH ANCHOVY CRUMBS

Winning the tricky Spanish invention test was Danielle's favourite moment in the series. She inherited a basket of lamb and anchovies from Mat (who had a disaster with her dessert ingredients) and embraced the challenge. 'This dish danced a fandango on our tongues,' said Matt Preston. Danielle got a huge round of applause from the kitchen.

2.5kg leg of lamb, boned
TEMPRANILLO REDUCTION
375ml (1½ cups) tempranillo*
2 red onions, finely diced
LAMB REDUCTION
1 tbs olive oil
1 leek, sliced
1 carrot, peeled, diced
1 tbs smoked sweet paprika

1 tbs hot paprika
2 white anchovies, chopped
250ml (1 cup) tempranillo
LAMB & BEAN CASSEROLE
1–2 tbs olive oil
½ red onion, chopped
6 cloves garlic, chopped
1 tbs smoked sweet paprika
125ml (½ cup) tempranillo

400g can diced tomatoes
400g can cannellini beans, drained, rinsed
1 tbs aged sherry vinegar
ANCHOVY CRUMBS
2 cloves garlic, finely chopped
4 white anchovies, finely chopped
80g dried breadcrumbs

1 Trim the lamb and cut into 3cm chunks. Keep 250g chopped off-cuts for the lamb reduction.

2 To make tempranillo reduction, put wine and onions in a small saucepan and bring to the boil. Cook for 10 minutes or until reduced. Strain and reserve.

3 To make lamb reduction, preheat oven to 180°C. Heat oil in an ovenproof frying pan over medium heat and cook leek and carrot, stirring often, for 10 minutes or until caramelised. Transfer to a bowl. Increase heat to high, add lamb off-cuts to pan and cook for 5 minutes or until well browned. Return leek and carrot to pan with paprika and anchovies. Deglaze pan with wine and cook for 5 minutes or until reduced by half. Add 250ml (1 cup) water and bring to the boil. Transfer to oven and roast for 10 minutes. Strain liquid through a sieve and set aside.

4 To make lamb and bean casserole, heat 1 tbs oil in a large saucepan over high heat and cook lamb chunks in 5 batches, adding more oil if needed. Add onion, garlic and paprika, stirring to combine. Deglaze pan with tempranillo, then stir in tempranillo reduction, lamb reduction and tomatoes. Cover and bring to the boil, then reduce heat to low and simmer for 1½ hours or until lamb is tender.

5 Add cannellini beans and cook, uncovered, for 10 minutes or until reduced and thickened. Stir in sherry vinegar and transfer to a serving dish.

6 To make anchovy crumbs, preheat oven to 200°C. Using your fingers, rub garlic and anchovies through breadcrumbs. Spread onto an oven tray and bake for 3 minutes or until golden. Cool and sprinkle over casserole to serve.

TIP Tempranillo is a dry red wine, which originated in Spain but is now also produced in Australia.

Serves **6–8**
Preparation **1 hour**
Cooking **40 minutes**

Michael's
TAPAS OF LAMB THREE WAYS

'Walking up to the judges is always hard: I just want one of them to say something nice.'
Michael's lamb tapas certainly had them talking nicely: 'That salsa verde has a lovely
sweet-sour tang and works perfectly with the lamb,' said Matt Preston. George was thrilled:
'Michael, I knew when I set eyes on you in Adelaide that you were going to go a long way.'

2.5kg leg of lamb, boned, divided
   into 3 portions
ROAST ANCHOVY LAMB
1 tbs extra virgin olive oil
2 cloves garlic, crushed
2 anchovy fillets, finely chopped
2 tsp thyme leaves
1 lemon, zested
SALSA VERDE
50g (¼ cup) salted capers,
   rinsed, chopped
¼ cup mint leaves, chopped
¼ cup basil leaves, chopped
½ cup flat-leaf parsley, chopped

2 eschalots, finely chopped
60ml (¼ cup) extra virgin
   olive oil
2 tbs lemon juice
CUMIN-CRUSTED LAMB
2 tbs ground cumin
2 tbs ground paprika
2 tbs olive oil
OLIVE SALAD
150g kalamata olives, pitted,
   chopped
2 eschalots, diced
½ cup flat-leaf parsley, chopped
1 tbs lemon juice

1 tbs olive oil
100ml vegetable oil
50g (¼ cup) salted capers,
   rinsed
HARISSA LAMB
2 tbs harissa
10 anchovy fillets, chopped
1 tbs extra virgin olive oil
1 small red capsicum, sliced
1 clove garlic, crushed
1 tbs sherry vinegar
2 red capsicums, roasted, peeled,
   seeded
1 lemon, juiced

1 **To make roast anchovy lamb,** preheat oven to 180°C. Take one portion of the lamb and
   butterfly it to lie flat. Mix together olive oil, garlic, anchovies, thyme and lemon zest and season
   with salt and pepper. Coat lamb with the mixture. Preheat a barbecue or chargrill pan over high
   heat and cook meat for 3 minutes each side or until grill marks appear. Transfer to a roasting
   pan and roast for 15 minutes for medium–rare or until cooked to your liking. Cover loosely with
   foil and rest for 15 minutes, then slice.
2 **To make salsa verde,** combine all the ingredients and season.
3 **For cumin-crusted lamb,** cut one portion of lamb into 2cm cubes. Toss in combined cumin and
   paprika. Heat oil in a frying pan over medium heat and cook lamb for 7 minutes until browned.
4 **To make olive salad,** combine olives, eschalots, parsley, lemon juice and olive oil. Season. Heat
   vegetable oil in a small saucepan over high heat. Cook capers for 2 minutes until crisp. Remove
   with a slotted spoon and drain on paper towel.
5 **For harissa lamb,** combine harissa and anchovies. Slice remaining lamb into small steaks and
   coat with mixture. Heat half the oil in a frying pan and cook sliced capsicum and garlic over
   medium heat for 3 minutes or until tender. Stir in sherry vinegar and set aside. Blend roasted
   capsicums with lemon juice until smooth, season and set aside. Heat remaining oil in a frying
   pan over medium heat and cook lamb steaks for 2 minutes each side.
6 Serve roast anchovy lamb slices with salsa verde. Arrange cumin-crusted lamb on olive salad,
   topped with fried capers. Serve harissa lamb on sautéed capsicum with capsicum sauce.

Chef Martin Boetz's
THAI-BRAISED MURRAY COD WITH CRISP CHILLI & GARLIC RELISH

FISH STOCK
2kg white-fleshed fish bones
100g ginger
4 coriander roots with stems
5 spring onions
BRAISED MURRAY COD
4 coriander roots, scraped
3 cloves garlic, peeled
5cm piece ginger, peeled
½ tsp white peppercorns
2 star anise
50ml cold-pressed canola oil
100ml Chinese rice wine
    (shaoxing)

50g rock sugar, finely pounded
150ml oyster sauce
75ml light yellow bean soy sauce
30ml kecap manis
1 cinnamon quill
150g Chinese winter melon,*
    peeled, cut into 3cm pieces
1kg Murray cod, cleaned, scaled
5cm piece ginger, cut into
    julienne
CHILLI & GARLIC RELISH
5cm piece ginger
6 cloves garlic
50g eschalots

250ml (1 cup) canola oil
10g dried red chillies, seeded
2 tsp sea salt
1 tbs sugar
GARNISH
4cm piece ginger, cut into
    julienne
50g Asian celery leaves,*
    shredded
3 spring onions, green part only,
    thinly sliced
1 long red chilli, thinly sliced

1 To make fish stock, preheat oven to 150°C. Put fish bones and 2L water in a large saucepan. Bring to the boil over low–medium heat and skim any froth from the surface. Add ginger, coriander and spring onions, simmer for 20 minutes, then strain.

2 For braised cod, pound coriander roots, garlic, ginger, peppercorns and 1 star anise to a smooth paste with a mortar and pestle. Heat oil in a large saucepan over medium–high heat, add paste and fry for 4 minutes or until fragrant.

3 Deglaze pan with rice wine. Add rock sugar, oyster sauce, yellow bean soy sauce, kecap manis and 1.75L fish stock. Bring to the boil and skim surface. Adjust seasoning to a balance of sweet, aromatic and salty. Add cinnamon quill and remaining star anise, then set aside.

4 Steam winter melon in a bamboo steamer over boiling water for 10 minutes or until tender.

5 Place fish in a large deep roasting pan and arrange winter melon around fish. Cover fish with stock mixture, cover with a sheet of baking paper, then with a sheet of foil and bake for 50 minutes or until cooked through. Leave to rest, covered, for 10 minutes.

6 To make chilli & garlic relish, use a mortar and pestle to separately pound ginger, garlic and eschalots to a paste. Heat oil in a wok to 160°C (see cooking notes, page 264). Fry each paste separately until crisp, remove with a slotted spoon and drain on paper towel. Fry chillies for 5–10 seconds only (they will colour quickly), remove and drain, keeping oil. Use a mortar and pestle to pound all fried ingredients together into a paste. Mix in salt, sugar and 50ml of the oil.

7 Lift fish out of liquid and into serving dish. Arrange winter melon around fish.

8 Pour braising liquid into a saucepan and bring to a simmer. Add julienned ginger and season. Spoon enough liquid over fish to half cover. Garnish with Asian celery leaves, spring onion, chilli and ginger. Serve with chilli and garlic relish.

TIP Chinese winter melon and Asian celery leaves are available from Asian greengrocers.

Chef Nigella Lawson's
ROAST BEEF DINNER

Nigella described the Gen X team's perfectly cooked beef as 'fantastic'. 'It's hard to cook simple things well because there are no flourishes to hide behind when things go wrong.' It's also hard to cook simple things well when you're allowed in the kitchen for only 20 minutes and then have one minute to brief the next team member on what's happening!

2kg standing rib roast (6 cutlets)
2 tbs olive oil
HORSERADISH SAUCE
250g (1 cup) Greek yoghurt
160ml (2/3 cup) double cream
1/2 tsp sea salt

1/3 cup grated fresh
　horseradish
1 tsp Dijon mustard
2 tsp white wine vinegar
1/2 cup chopped chives

YORKSHIRE PUDDINGS
330ml (11/3 cups) milk
4 eggs
1/2 tsp salt
250g (12/3 cups) plain flour

1 Preheat oven to 200°C. Brush rib roast with oil and season well with salt and pepper. Place in a roasting pan and roast for 50 minutes for medium–rare, or to your liking. Cover loosely with foil and leave for 20 minutes before carving. Reserve 3 tsp dripping from pan.
2 **Meanwhile, to make horseradish sauce,** beat together yoghurt, cream, salt, horseradish, mustard and vinegar. Stir in chives just before serving.
3 **To make Yorkshire puddings,** increase oven to 220°C. Whisk together milk, eggs, salt and flour until smooth. Leave to stand for 15 minutes.
4 Place 1/4 tsp of the beef dripping into each hole of a 12-hole (80ml/1/3-cup) muffin pan and heat in the oven for 10 minutes. Pour batter into hot muffin pan and cook for 15 minutes until puddings are puffed and golden brown. Serve immediately with beef and horseradish sauce.

CREAMY POTATO GRATIN

2kg floury potatoes, peeled
500ml (2 cups) milk
500ml (2 cups) thickened cream

1 onion, peeled, left whole
2 cloves garlic, crushed
50g unsalted butter

1 Preheat oven to 240°C and grease a 2L deep ovenproof dish.
2 Cut potatoes into 1cm-thick slices and put in a large saucepan with milk, cream, onion, garlic and 1 tsp salt. Bring to a simmer and cook for 15 minutes or until tender. Remove the onion.
3 Pour potato mixture into the dish. Dot with butter and bake for 20 minutes or until browned and bubbly on top.

Chef Nigella Lawson's
RED VELVET CUPCAKES

Dani did her best to save the day for the youthful red team. The cupcakes she found in the oven were sunken and burnt to a crisp. 'I'm so stressed right now, I don't know what to do,' she said. What she did do was cook up a whole new batch of cupcakes. 'I think we all owe Dani a great debt of gratitude,' said Shannon. 'Those cupcakes look fantastic.'

250g (1²/₃ cups) plain flour
2 tbs dark (Dutch) cocoa*
2 tsp baking powder
½ tsp bicarbonate of soda
100g unsalted butter, softened
220g (1 cup) caster sugar
2 eggs

1 tbs red food colouring paste*
2 tsp vanilla bean paste
180ml (³/₄ cup) buttermilk
1 tsp cider or white vinegar
ICING
125g cream cheese, at room
   temperature, chopped

125g unsalted butter, softened
500g icing sugar, sifted
1 tsp lemon juice
Chocolate shavings and red
   sanding sugar,* to decorate

1 Preheat oven to 170°C. Line eighteen 80ml (¹/₃-cup) muffin holes with paper cases.
2 Sift flour, cocoa, baking powder and bicarbonate of soda into a bowl.
3 Using an electric mixer, beat butter and sugar until pale and fluffy. Add eggs, one at a time, beating well after each addition. Add food colouring and vanilla and beat until well combined.
4 Gently fold in half the flour and cocoa mixture. Combine buttermilk and vinegar and fold in, then fold in remaining flour and cocoa until just combined. Spoon into the paper cases.
5 Bake for 20 minutes or until cakes spring back to a gentle touch. Transfer to a wire rack to cool.
6 **To make the icing,** put cream cheese, butter, icing sugar and lemon juice in a food processor, and process until smooth. Spread over cooled cupcakes and decorate with chocolate shavings and red sanding sugar.

TIP **Dark (Dutch) cocoa** is available from good delis. **Red food colouring paste** gives a much more intense colour than food colouring liquid from the supermarket. It is available from cake decorating supply shops or online. **Sanding sugar** is also available from cake decorating supply shops or online. Alternatively, rub red food colouring paste into white sugar.

Serves **8**
Preparation **30 minutes**
Cooking **45 minutes**

Rachel's
CHOCOLATE CAKE THAT NIGELLA LOVED

Rachel and Kate went a long way towards winning the 'tag-team' challenge for the Gen X 'oldies'. 'I'm just going to make my fail-safe chocolate cake,' Rachel decided, when Kate told her a cake was needed. When she realised she was serving her everyday recipe to the Domestic Goddess, she was nervous: 'It looks fudgy, but it's just a cake I make all the time.'

125g unsalted butter, softened
220g (1 cup) caster sugar
3 eggs
1 tsp vanilla bean paste

150g (1 cup) plain flour
25g (¼ cup) dark (Dutch) cocoa*
2 tsp baking powder

GANACHE ICING
150g dark chocolate (70% cocoa solids), chopped
250g unsalted butter, chopped

1 Preheat oven to 180°C. Grease a 20cm round cake pan and line base with baking paper. Using an electric mixer, beat butter and sugar until pale and fluffy. Add eggs, one at a time, beating well after each addition. Add vanilla and beat well.

2 Sift flour, cocoa and baking powder over butter mixture and stir to combine. Add 125ml (½ cup) boiling water and mix well.

3 Pour into cake pan. Bake for 45 minutes until cake is risen and firm to a gentle touch. Cool in pan for 5 minutes, then turn out onto a wire rack to cool completely.

4 To make ganache icing, fill a small saucepan one-third full with water and bring to a gentle simmer. Place chocolate and butter in a small heatproof bowl, place over pan and stir until melted (don't let the bowl touch the water). Set aside for 15 minutes or until cooled and thickened slightly. Spread over cake and refrigerate until set.

TIP **Dark (Dutch) cocoa** is available from good delis.

'This chocolate cake is a knock-out, completely fabulous. I'll have the recipe, please!' Nigella

OMG MOMENTS

The teams crash from one 'oh-my-God' moment to the next. Neil Perry's Qantas challenge has them gibbering with panic, and the elimination that follows has everyone gibbering with excitement. 'Heston's in the house and it's burger day,' shouts George, but burger day is Rachel's last. Alana shines in the Greenhouse. Shannon shines, too, but it's still time to leave.

FILMING DIARY

Sunday

EPISODE 37 Plate up 27 perfect portions of Neil Perry's Qantas first-class food.

Monday

EPISODE 38 It's Heston's elimination test and everyone wants to make burgers.

Tuesday

EPISODE 39 Gary gets down on his knees in awe as Kate almost wins immunity.

Wednesday

EPISODE 40 Which team can make great food without making environmental mess?

Thursday

EPISODE 41 Shannon and Craig confuse the judges with their elimination dishes.

Friday

EPISODE 42 Masterclass is warming and George cooks with just one ingredient.

Week 7

SERIOUS PRESSURE

'I'd like to say I love the energy in the room,' says Gary. 'But, frankly, it's bordering on panic.' Of course it's bordering on panic: the Top 16 have been put into pairs and have one hour to cook 27 portions of a Neil Perry first-class Qantas dish. In case that wasn't enough pressure, Matt Preston has invited chefs Thomas Keller and Andoni Aduriz to help judge. 'Even I'm scared now,' admits Gary.

Thomas Keller is Michael's hero: 'In my wildest dreams I don't think I could've conjured up meeting him.'

'I hope your dish is going to wow him,' says Matt Preston. Michael and Shannon are cooking the syrup sponge. 'This is a piece of cake,' says Michael, in an ominous and obvious premonition of disaster.

Danielle is told to show her snapper 'more love'. The fish–love strategy pays off and she and Kate win the challenge.

Below: Billy decides he'd like 'anything except the beef' in the Qantas challenge and Mat has had disasters with steak since the Mean Fiddler. Of course, they get the meat. Within minutes, Neil Perry notices they're in 'serious beef bother'.

A BRAVE GREEN WORLD

'One man's trash is another man's treasure,' says Gary, cryptically. Circular Quay's Greenhouse restaurant welcomes the teams and challenges them to make great food without making a mess of the environment. Six fabulous dishes must be served to a selection of 'green foodies'. But, if the teams need flour, they must mill it themselves. If they want butter, they need to get churning. Sun is blue team captain but 'there's no-one at the wheel of this vehicle,' says team-member Peter.

'I just want the ground to open up and swallow me,' says Sun, as a chaotic service starts. 'Nothing's ready.' But she has a master plan. Peter, 'the original sell-ice-to-eskimos man', and Hayden are sent onto the floor to win votes. Surely Hayden's team-loss curse has to end soon? It does... Sun's blues win in a surprise landslide.

Clockwise from below: Michael, Shannon, Rachel and Craig can't contain their excitement at the 'best elimination challenge ever'; Dani's idol, Luke Nguyen, is impressed by her Vietnamese beef; Greenhouse chef Matt Stone weighs the waste and the blue team wins an extra 10 points.

'Michael's got this slightly psychotic look on his face.'
Heston Blumenthal

HESTON'S IN THE HOUSE

'Ladies and gentlemen, this is your OMG moment,' says Matt Preston, as Heston Blumenthal strides into the MC kitchen. Matt describes the reaction as a bit like Madonna arriving. 'I'll take that as a compliment,' says Heston, kindly. 'This is the best elimination ever,' sighs Shannon.

Everyone on the balcony suffers serious elimination envy as Heston's 'perfection burger' and fries are revealed to Michael, Shannon, Rachel and Craig. 'Great, we're doing dessert,' thinks Craig, suspiciously.

Michael loves the challenge, but the meat mixer and Shannon 'aren't friends'. Craig makes a burger that is bigger than Heston's head, and Rachel is so far out of her depth she's drowning. 'You're a very nice man, Heston,' she says, 'but slightly evil.' She gets her meats muddled up, but leaves with her sense of humour intact.

Chef Neil Perry's
CRAB & FENNEL SALAD
WITH GARLIC CREME FRAICHE

Dani and Sun were chosen to cook as a team in the Qantas challenge. 'Sun and I both have strong personalities,' said Dani, candidly. 'I'm sort of glass half-full. Sun might be sort of glass half-empty.' Dani impressed the judges by taking on the immense task of preparing 27 portions of crab for this delicately flavoured salad of Neil Perry's.

GARLIC CREME FRAICHE
3 cloves garlic, unpeeled
45g (1/3 cup) slivered almonds
120g (1/2 cup) crème fraîche
1 lemon, zested, juiced
CRAB & FENNEL SALAD
1 large bulb fennel

350g cooked blue swimmer or
   mud crab meat*
160g (2 cups) thinly shredded
   savoy cabbage
2 tbs chopped flat-leaf parsley
200g marinated artichoke hearts,
   drained, halved

DRESSING
60ml (1/4 cup) extra virgin
   olive oil
1 tbs red wine vinegar

1 To make garlic crème fraîche, preheat oven to 180°C. Wrap garlic cloves together in foil and place on an oven tray. Place almonds, uncovered, on a sheet of foil at other end of tray. Roast for 10 minutes or until almonds are golden. Remove almonds with foil and set aside. Return garlic to oven and roast for 10 minutes or until garlic is soft. Cool for 5 minutes. Squeeze garlic from skins and pound to a smooth paste, using a mortar and pestle. Combine paste with crème fraîche, zest and half the lemon juice. Season with salt and pepper.

2 To make crab and fennel salad, trim fennel, then thinly shave with a mandolin or sharp knife. Place in a large bowl and toss with remaining lemon juice to prevent browning. Pick over crab meat to remove any shell, then add to fennel with cabbage, parsley and artichokes. Season.

3 To make dressing, combine oil and vinegar in a bowl. Season, then whisk until emulsified. Pour over salad and toss gently. Scatter salad with almonds and serve with garlic crème fraîche.

TIP **Cooked, picked crab meat** is available from selected fishmongers. Alternatively, buy whole cooked crabs and pick out the meat.

Makes **6**
Preparation **30 minutes + 1½ hours refrigeration**
Cooking **1 hour**

Chef Neil Perry's
CARAMELISED LEEK & GOAT'S CHEESE TARTS

Craig and Rachel worked as a team on the Qantas tarts. They had to make 27 portions and found the pastry very labour intensive. 'Think positive,' instructed Rachel, as time ran away from them. 'I am doing,' said Craig. 'I'm positive they won't come out!' They did come out, but the pastry was rather more 'rustic' and thick than Neil Perry's version.

SHORTCRUST PASTRY
450g (3 cups) plain flour
225g cold butter, chopped
FILLING
70g butter, chopped
1 tbs olive oil

3 small leeks, white part only, thinly sliced
1 clove garlic, finely chopped
80ml (⅓ cup) dry white wine
80ml (⅓ cup) vegetable stock
2 tbs finely chopped sage

1 tbs finely chopped flat-leaf parsley
2 eggs, plus 2 egg yolks, extra
200ml pouring cream
120g soft goat's cheese, crumbled

1 To make pastry, process flour and butter in a food processor until mixture resembles breadcrumbs. Add 60ml (¼ cup) chilled water and process until pastry comes together. Shape into 6 discs, wrap in plastic wrap and refrigerate for 30 minutes.
2 Roll out pastry discs on a lightly floured surface until 3mm thick. Ease pastry into six 12cm (3cm-deep) tart pans with removable bases. Trim edges and lightly prick bases. Refrigerate for 1 hour.
3 Preheat oven to 180°C. Line tart shells with baking paper, fill with dried beans or rice and place on an oven tray. Bake for 20 minutes, then remove beans and paper. Bake for a further 10 minutes or until pastry is dry and pale golden. Cool.
4 Meanwhile, to make filling, heat butter and oil in a frying pan over medium heat. Add leeks, garlic and ½ tsp salt and cook, stirring occasionally, for 15 minutes or until leeks are soft and starting to caramelise. Add wine and simmer for 2 minutes or until almost evaporated. Add stock and simmer for a further 5 minutes or until almost evaporated. Season with pepper and transfer to a bowl. Cool, then stir in sage and parsley. Divide among tart shells.
5 Whisk eggs, yolks and cream together in a jug and pour into tart shells until almost full. Scatter tarts evenly with goat's cheese. Bake for 20 minutes or until just set and serve warm.*

TIP Tarts can be made a day in advance and stored in an airtight container in the fridge. **Reheat** in a 180°C oven just before serving.

Chef Heston Blumenthal's
PERFECTION BURGER

TOMATO KETCHUP

1.5kg very ripe tomatoes, halved

1 tsp mustard powder

1 pinch ground cloves

PATTIES

600g short-rib meat

300g beef brisket

125g Wagyu beef (marble 8+)

300g chuck steak, chilled, cut
   into 3cm cubes

3 tsp salt

120g butter

8 brioche or burger buns

8 slices Swiss cheese

Grape seed oil, to shallow-fry

1¹/₂ tbs maple syrup

1¹/₂ tbs Bundaberg rum

3 tsp sherry vinegar

French mustard, mayonnaise,
   iceberg lettuce, tomato, onion
   rings and pickles, to serve

1 **To make tomato ketchup,** place tomatoes in large saucepan. Cover and bring to the boil over medium heat. Cook, covered, for 20 minutes or until very soft and pulpy. Press through a very coarse sieve, discard solids and pour liquid into a deep frying pan. Bring to a simmer over medium heat. Stir in mustard and cloves and cook for 20 minutes. Reduce heat to low–medium and cook for 15 minutes, stirring often or until thick and ketchup-like. Season with a little salt.

2 **To make patties,** cut short-rib, brisket and Wagyu into 3cm cubes and toss together. Using a meat grinder with a 3mm plate, grind combined meats twice. Transfer to a bowl and refrigerate for 45 minutes or until very cold.

3 Combine cubed chuck steak, cold ground meats and salt and mix well. Place two layers of plastic wrap over a chopping board or on an oven tray and position under mouth of grinder. Using an 8mm plate, pass meat mixture through the grinder. This will retain some larger pieces of the chuck steak. Try to keep the individual strands running lengthwise in the same direction without getting them tangled together – start laying the meat down at the edge of the sheet furthest from the grinder and work across to the closest edge. Wrap the meat up tightly in the plastic wrap, twisting the ends in opposite directions to form a log. Prick a few holes in it with a skewer to release any air pockets, then continue to twist the ends to tighten until the log is about 10cm in diameter and 24cm long. Wrap the log in another layer of plastic wrap to prevent it coming apart and refrigerate for 45 minutes or until chilled.

4 Cut wrapped log into 8 slices. Remove plastic, take each slice between the palms of your hands and press into a patty 2cm thick and same size as bun, keeping the grain of the meat running in the same direction. Place on a tray and cover with plastic wrap. Refrigerate until required.

5 Put butter in a saucepan and cook over medium heat until melted. Pour into a jug and leave for solids to settle, then pour off liquid into bowl and discard solids. Preheat a grill to high, cut buns in half and brush cut sides with clarified butter. Grill for 2 minutes or until lightly toasted. Place a slice of cheese onto each bun base.

6 Heat a large frying pan over high heat until very hot. Add grape seed oil and cook the patties in 2 batches for 2 minutes, turning every 30 seconds, until evenly seared. Remove patties and deglaze pan with maple syrup and rum. Add a pinch of salt and sherry vinegar and simmer for 30 seconds. Return patties to pan in 2 batches to coat with glaze.

7 Place bun bases under hot grill to melt cheese. Spread with tomato ketchup, mustard and mayonnaise. Top with lettuce, tomato, onions, patties, pickles and bun tops.

'How do you make a hamburger smile?
Pickle it gently.' Gary (accompanied by groans)

Chef Heston Blumenthal's
TRIPLE-COOKED CHIPS

'Listen to the sound of those chips – that's the sound of crispy,' said Gary, and Heston agreed. Cooking with Heston was Michael's best moment of the series. He made a crazy lime milkshake that smoked with liquid nitrogen and reminded him of going to the milkbar with his Dad. 'Michael brought fun, energy and passion to this challenge,' said Heston.

1.5kg desiree potatoes, peeled
Grape seed oil, to deep-fry
Table salt and sea salt, to serve

1 Cut the potatoes into chips about 1.5cm thick. (Don't worry too much about making them all the same size, the variation will give a greater range of textures.) As soon as the chips are cut, put them in a colander under cold running water for 2 minutes to rinse off some of the starch, then drain.

2 Bring a large saucepan of salted water to the boil (10g salt per 1L water). Add the chips and return to the boil. Reduce the heat and simmer gently for 8 minutes or until the chips are cooked through and have just begun to break up but are not falling apart (the fissures that form in the potato trap the fat, creating a crunchy crust).

3 Using a slotted spoon, carefully lift the potatoes out of the water. Leave on a wire rack for 10 minutes to cool slightly, then refrigerate for 30 minutes or until cold.*

4 Fill a deep-fryer or large saucepan one-third full with oil and heat over medium heat to 130°C (see cooking notes, page 264). Cook the chips in 4 batches for 6 minutes or until they have a dry appearance and are just slightly coloured. Drain well, then cool on a wire rack for 10 minutes, then refrigerate for 35 minutes or until cold.

5 Preheat oven to 160°C. Reheat the oil to 190°C. Cook the chips in 4 batches for 4 minutes or until crisp and golden brown. Drain well and season with a mixture of table salt and sea salt. Keep warm in the oven while you cook the remaining chips.

TIP **Cooling the chips** right down between each stage of cooking eliminates most of the moisture that otherwise escapes from the chips as steam during frying, making them soggy. Instead, you'll have a crisp crust and a fluffy centre – the perfect chip. The dry air of the fridge is the perfect environment to evaporate excess moisture.

Alana's
PEACH SPICED CRUMBLE WITH
ORANGE BLOSSOM CREME

Alana added spices to Kate's leftover pizza dough and came up with this challenge-winning dish that Greenhouse chef Matt Stone added to his menu.

8 peaches
200g butter
250ml (1 cup) rosé verjuice
PIZZA DOUGH
1 tsp dried yeast
1 tsp honey
250g (1²/₃ cups) plain flour
1 tbs olive oil

ORANGE BLOSSOM CREME
400g crème fraîche
2 tbs mascarpone
1 tbs orange blossom water
CRUMBLE
4 cinnamon quills
1 whole nutmeg, grated
2 tbs allspice

80ml (¹/₃ cup) honey
200g hazelnuts
200g walnuts
2 tbs orange zest
GLAZE
125ml (¹/₂ cup) orange juice
1 vanilla bean, split
2 tbs honey

1 Bring a large saucepan of water to the boil. Cut a small cross in the base of each peach. Blanch peaches in boiling water for 20 seconds then refresh immediately in cold water. Cool, then peel away skins. Halve peaches crosswise, remove stones and set aside.

2 For pizza dough, combine yeast and honey with 60ml (¹/₄ cup) lukewarm water in a small jug. Leave for 10 minutes until foamy. Sift flour and a pinch of salt into a large bowl and make a well in the centre. Add yeast mixture, olive oil and 80ml (¹/₃ cup) water. Mix to a soft dough and knead for 5 minutes or until smooth and elastic. Place in a lightly oiled bowl, cover and leave in a warm place to prove for 45 minutes or until doubled in size.

3 For orange blossom crème, mix together all ingredients, cover and refrigerate until required.

4 To make crumble, preheat oven to 190°C. Grind cinnamon, nutmeg and allspice in a spice grinder to a fine powder. Roll out pizza dough until 1cm thick and place on an oven tray. Rub half the spice mixture over the surface and drizzle with honey. Bake for 15 minutes or until crisp and golden. Spread hazelnuts and walnuts on an oven tray and bake for 10 minutes or until lightly golden. Cool dough and nuts.

5 To make glaze, put orange juice, vanilla bean and honey in a saucepan and stir over medium heat until honey is dissolved and mixture is smooth. Increase heat to high and cook for 8 minutes or until thick and syrupy. Brush the cut side of the fruit with glaze, keeping remaining glaze. Arrange on oven trays and bake for 10 minutes or until softened. Remove and cool.

6 Reduce oven to 140°C. Process dough and nuts in 2 batches until mixture resembles coarse crumbs. Transfer to an ovenproof dish and stir through orange zest and remaining spice mixture. Rub in 150g of the butter, spread out and bake for 15 minutes or until dry.

7 Add remaining butter to the glaze. Heat a large frying pan over medium–high heat and add one-third of the glaze. Place one-third of the peaches, cut-side-down, in the pan and cook for 2 minutes or until caramelised. Transfer to an oven tray, cut-side-up, and repeat with remaining peaches and glaze in 2 batches. Deglaze pan with verjuice and drizzle over peaches.

8 Increase oven to 180°C. Spoon crumble over peaches and bake for 5 minutes. Serve with spoonfuls of orange blossom crème.

Serves **4 as a light meal**
Preparation **15 minutes**
Cooking **15 minutes**

Craig's
THAI PRAWN CURRY

Despite Craig's 'great leadership and vision' at the Greenhouse restaurant, his red team lost badly and went into a 'cooking by numbers' elimination test. Craig and Shannon left the judges in a quandary over which of their two great dishes was the best. Craig's Thai prawns were magnificent enough to just beat Shannon's 'near perfect' French toast.

1 onion, roughly chopped
2 cloves garlic, chopped
2 red bird's-eye chillies, thinly sliced
2 tbs roughly chopped coriander, plus extra leaves, to serve

2 tbs palm sugar
2 tbs fish sauce
400ml can coconut cream
20 medium green king prawns,* peeled with tails intact
1 lime, juiced

Steamed rice and lime wedges, to serve

1 Process onion, garlic, chillies, coriander, sugar and 1 tbs fish sauce in a food processor until finely chopped. Transfer mixture to a large frying pan and cook, stirring, over high heat for 1 minute or until fragrant.
2 Stir in coconut cream and bring to the boil. Reduce heat to medium and simmer for 8 minutes or until mixture starts to thicken. Add prawns and cook, stirring, for a further 3 minutes or until just cooked. Add lime juice and remaining 1 tbs fish sauce, adjusting seasoning if necessary with a little more lime juice or fish sauce.
3 Scatter with extra coriander and serve with steamed rice and lime wedges.

TIP Alternatively, use 700g firm white fish fillets, cut into 3cm pieces, instead of the prawns.

'This is not a dish that's shy of flavour. This is a big smack in the mouth.' Matt Preston

Serves **4**
Preparation **20 minutes**
Cooking **35 minutes**

Shannon's
FRENCH TOAST WITH
ORANGE ROSEWATER SYRUP & FIGS

'If there's a chance I'm going home today, I want to make a dessert. I love desserts,' said Shannon. She and Craig threw the judges into confusion in the elimination test: 'You've not only put up the best two dishes of the challenge, but some of the best food we've seen this series.' Although Shannon cooked 'a near perfect dish', it was her time to go home.

45g (¹/₃ cup) pistachios	8 thick slices sourdough	ORANGE ROSEWATER SYRUP
220g (1 cup) caster sugar	baguette	4 oranges, juiced
5 egg yolks	2 tbs vegetable oil	110g (¹/₂ cup) caster sugar
300ml cream	30g butter	1¹/₂ tsp ground cinnamon
2 tsp vanilla bean paste	4 figs, halved	60ml (¹/₄ cup) rosewater

1 Cook pistachios in a dry frying pan over medium heat, shaking the pan regularly, for 3 minutes or until just fragrant and lightly roasted. Sprinkle 110g (¹/₂ cup) sugar over the pistachios and cook for a further 2 minutes, shaking the pan occasionally, until sugar melts over pistachios. Transfer to a lightly oiled oven tray to cool.

2 **For orange rosewater syrup,** combine orange juice, sugar, cinnamon and rosewater in a small saucepan. Stir without boiling over low heat until has sugar dissolved, then increase heat and bring to the boil. Cook for 15 minutes or until reduced and syrupy. Set aside until just warm.

3 Whisk the egg yolks, cream, vanilla and remaining sugar in a large shallow dish. Soak the bread in the egg mixture for 5 minutes each side. Heat the oil and butter in a large frying pan over medium heat. Cook the bread in batches for 3 minutes each side until golden brown. Remove from pan and keep warm.

4 Increase heat to medium–high and place the figs, cut-side-down, in the pan. Cook for 1 minute or until browned. Serve French toast topped with fig halves. Sprinkle with candied pistachios and drizzle with syrup.

'This French toast is magnificent...
caramelised on the outside and soft and
gooey in the centre.' George

EGG INTOLERANCE &
SUGAR INTOLERANCE

GREEK IS THE WORD

'Holy mackerel, who's got themselves in a pickle?' teases George. It's the David Chang Korean invention test – Danielle is raising Gary's blood pressure and Adam is trying to cook with a 'loofah'. Another Calombaris enters the kitchen – one who can keep George in his place. Billy loses his dessert crown to Michael; and Adam bows out, while Craig takes a bow.

FILMING DIARY

Sunday

EPISODE 43 Think Korean-style in the David Chang 'invention box' challenge.

Monday

EPISODE 44 Mary Calombaris brings Greek heart to an elimination test.

Tuesday

EPISODE 45 Hayden cooks roast pork and almost wins 'stereo' immunity pins.

Wednesday

EPISODE 46 Food-court food-fight with a twist... low-carb, low-salt burger anyone?

Thursday

EPISODE 47 The red team go 'in the round' and Craig takes his final bow.

Friday

EPISODE 48 Mary's back in the kitchen for masterclass and Gary cooks with lamb.

Week 8

KOREAN INVENTIONS

David Chang of New York's Momofuku restaurant strides into the kitchen, making Mat so excited he can barely speak. The challenge is a 'Korean-style invention box', using pork, beef or mackerel.

Adam thinks the lotus root looks like the loofah he uses to wash his back, Dani can't read the ingredient labels and Hayden's 'winging it'. Adam's technique is to try to look 'as Korean as possible'.

Mat makes a Korean-inspired carpaccio, then realises he's 'in the wrong country' – no matter, David loves his dish. Danielle reduces her sauce so much that Gary asks: 'Am I going to die of salt poisoning?'

But Hayden's is the standout dish. 'You have a lot of potential that I just did not see coming,' says David Chang, impressed.

'Just because he looks like a dopey surfer-boy, doesn't mean Hayden can't cook,' Dani points out.

Below: Billy rushes to choose 'dessert' in the 'food-court food-fight' challenge, then discovers it has to be made without sugar or eggs. He picks Michael to cook against. 'Dessert against Billy... why me?' groans Michael.

the choices prove to be tactical. Blue-team Billy chooses dessert, of course, and picks red-team Michael to cook against.

Red Mat chooses rotisserie against blue Danielle. 'Does he think I'm a weak cook? He shouldn't do,' she glares.

Blue Ellie picks fish and chips against Craig. 'Cook fish and chips? No problem,' says Craig. 'That's probably why I'm overweight. She's too thin; look at her!'

Red Alana picks blue Kumar to make pizza because he 'struggled with it' earlier. 'Do not tell Kumar he can't do something. He's going to get that point now if it kills him,' says Sun. Kumar does get the point, helping his blue team to victory.

Michael is sent to his sixth elimination test in a row, but it's Craig who goes out in style. 'You'll be pleased to hear I didn't cry once on television...' he reassures his family and friends. 'No: four times... a day!'

Below: 'I think I am a better cook than George,' says Mary. 'I think so, too,' agrees Gary. Danielle, Michael, Adam and Ellie face a pressure test with heart, cooking four Greek dishes. Mrs Calombaris has to be restrained from helping.

'Today you need to cook like a Calombaris.' George

SOMETHING ABOUT MARY

'Greek is the word. Make my mum proud,' orders George. Mary Calombaris brings four dishes and a lot of heart into the kitchen, and keeps George in his place. 'She's cute as anything,' says Hayden, who's on the balcony, helping Michael in another elimination. Ellie covers her bench in mess but 'there's a reason why they call her the Ellie-minator,' Matt P points out. Adam chooses to return to diving and let Danielle follow her dream. 'Some people aren't lucky enough to have one passion, but I've got two. It makes me very lucky.'

A CULINARY COLOSSEUM

The contestants are called to Westfield shopping centre. 'I don't think we're going there to shop,' says Sun, suspiciously.

The 'food-court food-fight' challenge is a gladiator-style battle. Teams take turns to choose a dish and a competitor, and

Serves **4**
Preparation **45 minutes**
Cooking **2 hours 10 minutes**

Hayden's
BRAISED PORK BELLY WITH PICKLED
VEGETABLES & STICKY RICE BALLS

BRAISED PORK BELLY
200g piece pork belly
1 tsp salt flakes
1 tsp white vinegar
2 tbs olive oil
2cm piece ginger, chopped
3 cloves garlic, smashed
1 nashi pear, cut into eighths
1¹/2 tsp Korean miso paste*
1 tsp spicy soybean paste*
2¹/2 tbs soy sauce
4 thin slices lotus root
50g Korean vermicelli noodles*

PICKLED VEGETABLES
180ml (³/4 cup) brown
   rice vinegar
1 tbs caster sugar
1 tbs dried Korean anchovies,*
   chopped
45g can anchovies, chopped
1 cucumber, very thinly sliced
10cm piece ginger, peeled, very
   thinly sliced diagonally
¹/2 daikon, peeled, cut into batons
1 long red chilli, seeded,
   thinly sliced

STICKY RICE BALLS
200g (1 cup) medium-grain rice,
   unrinsed
16 perilla leaves*
60ml (¹/4 cup) brown rice vinegar
1¹/2 tbs red bean paste*
TO SERVE
¹/2 Chinese cabbage (wombok),
   shredded
2 spring onions, thinly sliced
1 red chilli, finely chopped
1 bunch shimeji mushrooms
1 nashi pear, cut into thin rounds

1 For pork belly, preheat oven to 220°C. Remove pork skin; score skin, place on oven tray and rub salt and vinegar into skin. Roast for 20 minutes or until crisp. Cool; cut into 3cm pieces.
2 Meanwhile, heat olive oil in a large saucepan over medium–high heat. Cook pork belly, fat-side-down, for 10 minutes or until fat has rendered and meat begins to colour. Pour out rendered fat.
3 Add ginger, garlic, nashi pear, miso paste, soybean paste, soy sauce and enough water to just cover. Cover and bring to the boil, then reduce heat to very low and cook for 2 hours or until tender. Remove pork belly and cut into 1cm-thick slices. Strain liquid into a jug and discard solids. Keep warm.
4 Cook lotus root in boiling salted water for 5 minutes or until tender. Place noodles in a heatproof bowl and cover with boiling water. Soak for 5 minutes until soft; drain.
5 Meanwhile, for pickled vegetables, combine vinegar, sugar and anchovies and stir until sugar has dissolved. Place cucumber, ginger, daikon and chilli in liquid and leave for 30 minutes.
6 Meanwhile, to make rice balls, combine rice and 500ml (2 cups) water in a saucepan. Cover tightly and bring to the boil, then reduce heat to very low and cook for 12 minutes without removing lid. Remove from heat and leave, covered, for 8 minutes or until rice is tender and all the water has been absorbed. Spread over an oven tray to cool.
7 Lay perilla leaves on a serving plate. Take heaped tablespoons of rice and roll into balls, using wet hands. Make a small indent in the top of each ball and drizzle with 1 tsp vinegar. Roll ¹/2 teaspoonfuls of red bean paste into balls and place onto rice balls.
8 To serve, arrange pork on a bed of noodles and wombok. Top with lotus root, spring onions, chilli and mushrooms and a little braising liquid. Scatter with slices of nashi pear and pork crackling. Serve sticky rice balls with pickled vegetables and a little pickling liquid.

TIP Korean miso paste (doenjang), **spicy soybean paste** (ssamjang), **Korean vermicelli** (jap chae), **dried Korean anchovies, red bean paste** and **perilla leaves** are available from Asian grocers.

Dani's
KOREAN RICE BURGER

Dani's 'wacky idea' was to make a dish that looked American but had Korean flavours. The 'bun' was made of rice; the sauce looked like tomato sauce, but wasn't! David Chang was impressed: 'Is it the most glamorous dish? No. But does it taste delicious? Absolutely!'

PICKLED VEGETABLES
60ml (¼ cup) brown rice vinegar
1 tbs caster sugar
½ daikon,* peeled, cut into julienne
¼ Chinese cabbage (wombok),* sliced
1 Lebanese cucumber, cut into ribbons
RICE BUNS
300g (1½ cups) medium-grain rice, unrinsed

80ml (⅓ cup) vegetable oil
35g (¼ cup) sesame seeds, toasted
PORK PATTIES
400g pork belly, skin removed
400g pork fillet
2 tsp ground white pepper
2 tsp caster sugar
1 tbs sesame oil
2 spring onions, finely chopped
2 tbs light soy sauce
2 cloves garlic, crushed

Vegetable oil, to shallow-fry
SAUCE
1½ tbs Korean chilli bean paste*
1½ tsp Korean miso paste*
2½ tbs kim chi liquid*
1 tsp sesame oil

1 **To make pickled vegetables,** combine vinegar, 2 tsp salt, sugar and 60ml (¼ cup) water in a jug. Put daikon and wombok in one bowl and cucumber in another. Pour half the pickling liquid into each bowl and leave for 30 minutes.

2 **To make rice buns,** put rice and 500ml (2 cups) water in a saucepan. Cover tightly and bring to the boil, then reduce heat to very low and cook for 12 minutes without removing lid. Remove from heat and leave, covered, for 8 minutes or until rice is tender and water has been absorbed.

3 Lightly oil a 10cm (2cm-deep) ring mould on a tray. Place one-eighth of cooked rice into mould and press to make a neat round. Remove mould and make another 7 buns. Chill for 15 minutes.

4 **To make pork patties,** trim fat from pork belly. Cut belly and pork into 3cm pieces. Push through a mincer set at the largest blade, or process in short bursts in a food processor. Add remaining ingredients and 1 tsp salt and combine until sticky.

5 To cook rice buns, heat oil in a large frying pan over medium heat. Cook rice buns in 2 batches for 3 minutes on each side or until crisp and golden. Cool slightly and carefully press sesame seeds onto both sides to lightly coat.

6 **To make sauce,** mix together all ingredients.

7 Divide pork mixture into 4 portions and shape into patties. Heat a little oil in a frying pan and cook patties over medium heat for 5 minutes each side or until cooked through.

8 Spread a spoonful of sauce over half the rice buns. Place patties on buns and top with pickled vegetables and another rice bun.

TIP Daikon and **Chinese cabbage (wombok)** are available from most greengrocers and supermarkets. **Kim chi liquid** is the pickling liquid in a container of kim chi. **Korean chilli bean paste, Korean miso paste** (doenjang) and **kim chi** are available from Asian grocers.

Mrs Calombaris's
LAMB KOUPES WITH TZATZIKI

TZATZIKI
3 Lebanese cucumbers, peeled, halved lengthwise
3 cloves garlic, unpeeled
2 tbs extra virgin olive oil, plus extra, to drizzle
420g (1½ cups) Greek-style yoghurt

1 tbs lemon juice
1 tbs finely chopped dill, plus extra, to serve
KOUPES
320g (2 cups) medium burghul*
75g (½ cup) plain flour
2 tbs olive oil
250g minced lamb

1 onion, finely chopped
½ tsp ground cinnamon
80g (½ cup) blanched almonds, roasted, finely chopped
½ cup flat-leaf parsley, finely chopped
Vegetable oil, to deep-fry
Lemon wedges, to serve

1 **To make tzatziki,** using a small spoon, scoop out cucumber seeds and discard. Coarsely grate cucumber into a bowl; toss with ½ tsp salt. Transfer to a colander placed over the bowl (make sure colander isn't sitting in the liquid in base of bowl) and refrigerate for 2 hours.

2 Meanwhile, preheat oven to 180°C. Place garlic on a doubled sheet of foil, drizzle with a little extra oil, then wrap garlic in the foil. Roast for 40 minutes or until soft. Cool slightly. Squeeze garlic from skins and mash with a fork.

3 Place garlic, oil, yoghurt, lemon juice and dill in a bowl. Squeeze moisture from cucumber, then add cucumber to bowl and stir together. Season with salt and pepper. Scatter with extra dill.

4 **Meanwhile, to make koupes,** put burghul and 375ml (1½ cups) boiling water in a heatproof bowl and soak for 2 hours. Process burghul, flour, ½ tsp salt and 60ml (¼ cup) water in a food processor for 30 seconds or until mixture forms a coarse-textured dough. Transfer to a bowl, cover, then rest for 15 minutes.

5 To make filling, heat olive oil in a frying pan over high heat. Add mince, breaking up with a wooden spoon, and cook, stirring occasionally, for 5 minutes or until starting to brown. Reduce heat to low, add onion and cook for 8 minutes or until onion is soft. Stir in cinnamon, almonds and parsley. Season with salt and pepper. Cool.

6 **To make croquettes,** using oiled hands, place 2 tbs dough in the palm of your hand and flatten to make an oval-shaped cup. Place 1 tbs filling in the centre, then bring up sides of dough to enclose. Seal edges, then roll into an oval croquette.* Repeat to make 20 croquettes.

7 Fill a deep-fryer or large saucepan one-third full with vegetable oil. Heat to 180°C (see cooking notes, page 264). Working in 4 batches, fry croquettes for 4 minutes or until golden. Remove with a slotted spoon and drain on paper towel. Season croquettes with salt and serve immediately with lemon wedges and tzatziki.

TIP Burghul (cracked wheat) is found in the health food section of supermarkets. **If the croquettes crack** when shaping, press the sides of the crack together evenly and pinch to seal.

'George has been well behaved since you've been here.' Adam

Michael's
BANANA MOUSSE TARTS

Billy chose to take on Michael in the 'food-court food-fight' challenge. He thought he could beat him at desserts, but Michael cooked up a surprise. 'Wow! Creamy, nutty, crunchy... who's the pastry king now?' said George, as Michael snatched Billy's crown. But Billy's blue team won and Michael had to cook his way out of his sixth elimination in a row.

PASTRY
110g cold unsalted butter, cubed
175g plain flour
60ml (¼ cup) pouring cream
MOUSSE
20g unsalted butter
1 large ripe banana, chopped

1 tsp caster sugar
½ tsp ground nutmeg
2 tsp gelatine powder
300ml pouring cream
TOPPINGS
20g unsalted butter
2 bananas, sliced diagonally

100g dark chocolate (70% cocoa solids), melted
100g blanched almonds, roasted, chopped

1 To make pastry, preheat oven to 180°C. Use your fingertips to rub butter into flour until mixture resembles fine breadcrumbs. Add cream and mix with a knife until mixture just comes together. Shape into a disc, wrap in plastic wrap and refrigerate for 30 minutes.

2 To make mousse, melt butter in a saucepan over medium heat and cook banana, sugar and nutmeg for 4 minutes or until caramelised, stirring occasionally; cool. Sprinkle gelatine over 2 tbs cold water in a small bowl. Leave for 1 minute to soften, then place in a dish of boiling water and whisk with a fork until dissolved. Cool slightly.

3 Place banana mixture, gelatine mixture and 60ml (¼ cup) of the cream in a blender. Blend to a thick purée. Beat the remaining cream to firm peaks. Gently fold together with banana mixture and refrigerate until required.

4 Roll out pastry between 2 sheets of baking paper to 3mm thick. Transfer to an oven tray and place a second tray on top. Bake for 10 minutes. Remove top tray and baking paper and bake for 5 minutes or until pastry is crisp and golden. Use a 10cm cutter to cut 4 rounds from the pastry. Transfer to a wire rack to cool.

5 To make toppings, melt butter in a frying pan. Add banana and cook over medium heat for 4 minutes or until caramelised. Place a lightly oiled 10cm ring mould over a round of pastry, fill with a layer of caramelised banana, keeping 8 slices for topping, and a drizzle of melted chocolate. Spoon in mousse and carefully remove ring.

6 Wash ring mould, re-oil and repeat with remaining ingredients to make 4 tarts. Decorate with caramelised banana, any remaining melted chocolate, and roasted almonds.

'He owns the dessert title now... Bow to him!' Billy

Serves **4**
Preparation **20 minutes**
Cooking **15 minutes**

Dani's VIETNAMESE BEEF NOODLE SALAD

Dani had a crisis of confidence before the 'in the round' elimination and was allowed to call her dad. 'You know what you've got to do. Just cook the best bloody tucker you've ever cooked in your life,' he told her. So Dani did. The judges loved the flavour of the beef, the crunch of the peanuts and the freshness of this salad, and she was into the Top 12.

500g sirloin steak, thinly sliced across the grain
100g rice vermicelli noodles
80ml (1/3 cup) vegetable oil, to shallow-fry
2 red eschalots, thinly sliced
1 cup coriander leaves
1 cup Thai basil leaves
2 carrots, cut into julienne
1 Lebanese cucumber, cut into long thin ribbons
1 long red chilli, thinly sliced
50g (1/3 cup) roasted unsalted peanuts, chopped

MARINADE
1 tbs oyster sauce
1 tbs soy sauce
1 clove garlic, crushed
1 tsp sesame oil

DRESSING
1 tbs fish sauce
2 tsp rice wine vinegar
1 tbs caster sugar
1 lime, juiced

1 **To make marinade,** mix all ingredients in a large glass bowl. Add the steak, toss together and leave to marinate until required.
2 **To make dressing,** combine all the ingredients and 1 tbs water in a small saucepan. Stir over low-medium heat for 3 minutes or until sugar has dissolved. Set aside to cool.
3 Cook the noodles in a saucepan of boiling water for 3 minutes or until tender. Drain, rinse under cold water and set aside in a colander to drain well.
4 Heat oil in a wok over medium heat and fry eschalots for 2 minutes or until golden. Lift out with a slotted spoon and drain on paper towel.
5 Drain all but 1 tbs oil from the wok, keeping the oil. Stir-fry steak in 4 batches over high heat for 1 minute or until browned, adding more oil when necessary.
6 Mix together noodles, herbs, vegetables and steak and toss with the dressing. Arrange on plates and top with chilli, peanuts and crisp eschalots.

Alana's
SPICED POACHED PEARS WITH
CHOCOLATE GANACHE & ORANGE CUSTARD

Alana's undercooked lamb took her into a second elimination round against Craig. 'If this is to be my last dish, I want to cook something from my heart,' said Alana, choosing the pears she poaches at home for her husband, Rob. She would've liked more time in the challenge to get the pears as beautifully soft as George wanted, so she's allowed longer cooking here.

POACHED PEARS
1.5L red wine
330g (1½ cups) caster sugar
Zest of 1 orange, cut into strips
3 star anise
2 cinnamon quills
1 vanilla bean, split, seeds scraped
6 josephine or beurre bosc pears, peeled

ORANGE CUSTARD
4 egg yolks
55g (¼ cup) caster sugar
1 vanilla bean, split, seeds scraped
1 orange, zested
250ml (1 cup) pouring cream
250ml (1 cup) milk
2 tbs Grand Marnier or other orange-flavoured liqueur

GANACHE
200g dark chocolate (70% cocoa solids), roughly chopped
150ml pouring cream
50g unsalted butter, chopped
MACADAMIA CRUMBLE
70g (½ cup) macadamias, roasted*
2 tbs caster sugar

1 **To poach pears,** combine wine, sugar, zest, spices and vanilla bean and seeds in a saucepan. Bring to the boil over high heat and cook for 1 minute or until sugar has dissolved. Add pears, adding extra water to submerge, if necessary. Lay a circle of baking paper, cut to the same size as the saucepan, on the surface of the liquid. Reduce heat to medium. Cook for 15 minutes or until pears are almost tender. Remove from heat and leave for 20 minutes; the residual heat will continue cooking pears. Refrigerate for 25 minutes or until completely cool.

2 **Meanwhile, to make custard,** whisk egg yolks, sugar, vanilla seeds and zest in a bowl until thick and pale. Place cream, milk and vanilla bean in a saucepan and bring almost to the boil. Whisking continuously, gradually add cream mixture to yolk mixture. Stir in liqueur. Return mixture to pan. Cook, stirring with a wooden spoon, for 8 minutes or until thick enough to coat back of spoon (do not boil). Strain through a fine sieve into a bowl. Cover and refrigerate for 30 minutes.

3 **To make ganache,** place chocolate, cream and butter in a heatproof bowl. Place over a saucepan of gently simmering water, then stir occasionally until melted and combined. Cool.

4 **To make macadamia crumble,** process macadamias and extra sugar in a food processor until finely chopped.

5 Spoon a little ganache onto each plate. Using a slotted spoon, remove the pears from syrup and place on ganache. Scatter with macadamia crumble and serve with orange custard.*

TIP To roast nuts, spread over an oven tray and bake at 180°C for 5 minutes. **Leftover custard and ganache** will keep in airtight containers in the fridge for up to 5 days.

'This custard is silky and thick with a beautiful orange flavour.' Gary

DOWN ON THE FARM

There are only two things on the menu at the Moran family farm: lamb and rocky road. Danielle's cold pasta sends her home this week, while Billy's immunity opponent takes a knitting break during their bake-off. Peter's red team serves a stodgy lunch and Ellie makes Gary cross in the 'stuffy versus fluffy' challenge. Artist Kumar is blindfolded and blind-sided.

FILMING DIARY

Sunday

EPISODE 49 The Top 12 hold a campfire cook-off to feed 200 at Jim Moran's farm.

Monday

EPISODE 50 Cold pasta sends Danielle home in the 'duck à l'orange' pressure test.

Tuesday

EPISODE 51 Billy needs every trick in the book, when he cooks against feisty Merle.

Wednesday

EPISODE 52 Corporate versus cocktail in the 'upstairs-downstairs' team challenge.

Thursday

EPISODE 53 It's a blindfold taste test and Kumar reveals his Achilles heel.

Friday

EPISODE 54 Ellie and Alana enjoy a New Zealand foodie reward tour.

Week 9

IT'S NO TIME TO BE SHEEPISH

Peter can't wait to get out of the city and spend time at Jim Moran's farm in the NSW Tablelands. This is a sheep farm and lamb is the dish of the day, to be cooked over an open fire. The first, daunting, task is the long race up the hillside to bring back a lamb carcass. 'Over your shoulder!' shouts George, as Kumar struggles, carrying his lamb like a baby.

Who was listening at masterclass when Gary showed how to butcher the whole lamb? Not Michael, who riskily decides to make rocky road instead.

A chill rain starts to fall as 200 hungry locals invade the paddock for lunch. Danielle's gnocchi are turned to mush on the open fire; Ellie's potatoes are like rocks; and the diners don't appreciate Peter's gorgeous lamb couscous. 'It was probably more suited to a picnic on Balmoral beach,' sighs Peter in the drizzle.

Below: Merle scolds Billy for poking holes in his cakes. Billy races along at MasterChef speed, spying on Merle through the screen to try to discover the secrets of her icing. She hides her icing, sits down to knit and messes with his mind.

make a rabbit terrine in 90 minutes?' asks Gary, curiously. 'We bought it,' admits Ellie. 'This is MasterChef; we don't buy stuff and chop it up,' says Gary, with an uncharacteristically cross expression.

The blue team are 'clean, organised and work really hard'. Peter's direction is 'brilliant', says Gary. But the meal they serve is too heavy. 'Out of the ashes of your kitchen chaos rose, phoenix-like, some great food,' says Matt P to Ellie, and the red team scrapes an amazing win.

KUMAR'S BRAIN FREEZE

'Being blindfolded has frozen part of my brain,' says Kumar the designer, as he struggles to identify ingredients in the taste test. He's optimistic: 'I'm pleased to have only four ingredients – less chance for mistakes.' But he's cooking against Michael, Billy and Peter and it's time to go.

Clockwise from below: A 'nightmare on lamb street' sends Danielle into an elimination test; Ellie's red team snatches victory from the jaws of defeat with great food at the 21st birthday party; Ellie and Alana ponder just how many things have been left off the shopping list for their party menu.

Who's going to get 'best in show' in the farm challenge?

MERLE MESSES WITH BILLY

Peter's wearing his first elimination apron: 'I know you hate it, but I think the black is very slimming,' says Billy, helpfully. The Ellie-minator rises to the occasion, but Danielle's duck pasta sends her home.

Billy battles against indomitable Merle in an old-school baking battle. 'I'd like that immunity pin for a souvenir,' says Merle competitively. This is a battle Billy can't win – Merle sits down to knit during the challenge, while Billy races in panic.

STUFFY OR FLUFFY?

The 'downstairs' blue team are serving a silver-service corporate lunch. The 'upstairs' reds cater a birthday party for 50 guests. Ellie takes a brief from twins celebrating their 21st birthday, but forgets vital ingredients on the shopping list and makes a horrible mistake. 'How did you

Billy's
LAMB CURRY WITH NAAN BREAD

Billy's lamb curry and rocky road dessert were 'best in show' and perfect for a cold wet day in the paddock of Jim Moran's farm. Billy's recipe makes a good large batch of curry to serve eight people. It's worthwhile making curry in bulk as it freezes so well.

1 tbs coriander seeds

1 tbs cumin seeds

2 tbs fennel seeds

1 tbs black peppercorns

2 tsp ground turmeric

2 x 1.4kg lamb shoulders, boned, cut into 4cm pieces

3 x 400ml cans coconut milk

2 x 400g cans chickpeas, rinsed, drained

CHILLI PASTE

10 long red chillies, chopped

6 stalks lemongrass, white part only, sliced

6 cloves garlic, chopped

4 onions, chopped

2 tbs olive oil

NAAN BREAD

300g (2 cups) plain flour

2 tsp baking powder

50g plain yoghurt

50g butter, melted

2 cloves garlic, finely chopped

1 Cook whole spices in a dry frying pan over medium heat for 3 minutes or until fragrant; cool. Using a mortar and pestle, grind spices to a powder. Add turmeric and pound until well combined. Rub over lamb and set aside.

2 To make chilli paste, process chillies, lemongrass, garlic and onions to a paste in a food processor. Heat oil in a large saucepan over medium heat and cook paste for 5 minutes or until fragrant. Add lamb and cook, stirring, until lightly browned and well coated in paste.

3 Add coconut milk, reduce heat to low and simmer, covered, for 45 minutes, stirring occasionally. Uncover and cook for a further 1 hour 15 minutes, stirring occasionally, until tender and liquid has reduced and thickened. Stir in the chickpeas and cook until heated through.

4 Meanwhile, to make naan bread, sift flour, baking powder and a pinch of salt into a large bowl. Make a well in the centre and add yoghurt and 150ml water. Mix to a sticky dough. Turn onto a floured work surface and knead for 1 minute or until smooth. Transfer to an oiled bowl and leave to rest for 30 minutes.

5 Roll dough into a cylinder and cut into 8 portions. Roll out each portion until 3mm thick. Mix together butter and garlic.

6 Heat a heavy-based pan over medium heat. Working one at a time, brush one side of naan bread with garlic butter. Place in pan, buttered-side-down, and brush top with garlic butter. Cook for 2 minutes on each side or until golden and cooked through. Wrap in foil to keep warm and repeat with remaining naan. Serve with the curry.

Michael's
ROCKY ROAD

Michael did the best job tactically at the Moran farm challenge. He hadn't paid attention to Gary's masterclass on how to butcher a lamb, so he concentrated instead on a sweet dessert to capture the children's votes. He took a huge risk and it paid off. In the last masterclass of the season, Matt Moran held a 'rocky road cook-off' against Billy and Michael.

150g dark chocolate, chopped
150g milk chocolate, chopped

90g (1 cup) marshmallows,
  halved

40g (¼ cup) sultanas
5 digestive biscuits, broken

1 Grease a 20cm square slice pan and line with baking paper, letting paper overhang two sides.
2 Fill a small saucepan one-third full with water and bring to a gentle simmer. Put chocolate in a heatproof bowl, place over pan and stir until melted (don't let the bowl touch the water).
3 Add remaining ingredients and fold together gently. Spread into pan and refrigerate for 15 minutes or until set. Cut or break into pieces to serve.

Billy's
ROCKY ROAD

While Michael's rocky road was traditional, Billy added fresh raspberries for tanginess. 'Michael, is your rocky road better than mine?' he shouted across the paddock. 'I beat you last week on desserts, mate,' Michael retorted, crushingly. 'Shut up!' screamed Billy. 'He's been crying every day since he lost his dessert crown to Michael,' Ellie said, quietly.

250g milk chocolate, chopped
40g butter
45g (1½ cups) puffed rice

45g (1 cup) mini marshmallows
125g raspberries

1 Grease an 18 x 28cm slice pan and line with baking paper, letting paper overhang two sides.
2 Fill a small saucepan one-third full with water and bring to a gentle simmer. Put chocolate in a heatproof bowl, place over pan and stir until melted (don't let the bowl touch the water).
3 Add remaining ingredients and fold together gently. Spread into pan and refrigerate for 15 minutes or until set. Cut or break into pieces to serve.

Ellie's

SZECHUAN-CRUSTED DUCK WITH ORANGE VINAIGRETTE & FENNEL SALAD

'Why can't Ellie cook like this in a team challenge?' asked George. The Ellie-minator came up trumps again with this elimination-test dish. 'This is the type of food I love to eat,' said George. Matt Preston was equally impressed: 'I like the crunch of the eschalots and the flavour of that vinaigrette. This is a very fine modern interpretation of a seventies classic.'

2 x 200g duck breast fillets
2 tsp ground Szechuan pepper*
60ml (¼ cup) vegetable oil
4 eschalots, thinly sliced
2 cloves garlic, thinly sliced
ORANGE VINAIGRETTE
2 tsp vegetable oil
1 eschalot, finely chopped
1 clove garlic, crushed
60ml (¼ cup) soy sauce

1 tbs mirin
125ml (½ cup) duck or chicken
  stock
3 oranges, zested, juiced
2 star anise
1 cinnamon quill
2 dried red chillies
1 tbs sugar
2 tbs lime juice
1 tbs olive oil

SALAD
1 baby fennel bulb, very thinly
  sliced, fronds reserved
2 oranges, segmented
1 long red chilli, seeded, cut into
  thin strips

1 Preheat oven to 180°C. Rub the duck all over with Szechuan pepper and season with salt. Score the skin. Heat a frying pan over low heat and cook the duck, skin-side-down, for 5 minutes or until the fat has rendered. Turn over and cook for 30 seconds. Place, skin-side-down, on an oven tray and roast for 5 minutes or until just cooked through. Cover loosely with foil and leave to rest.

2 Heat the oil in a wok over medium heat and cook the eschalots and garlic separately until crisp and golden. Remove with a slotted spoon and drain on paper towel.

3 **To make orange vinaigrette,** heat the oil in a saucepan over low–medium heat and cook the eschalot and garlic for 1 minute or until soft but not coloured. Add the soy sauce, mirin, stock, orange zest and juice, star anise, cinnamon, chillies and sugar. Bring to the boil, reduce the heat to medium and cook for 5 minutes or until reduced to a thick syrup. Strain and cool. Whisk in lime juice and olive oil. Season with salt and pepper.

4 **To make salad,** toss together fennel slices, orange segments, chilli and 1 tbs vinaigrette.

5 Arrange salad on plates. Slice the duck and arrange on top of the salad. Drizzle with remaining vinaigrette and sprinkle with crisp eschalots and garlic. Garnish with fennel fronds.

TIP Szechuan pepper is available from selected supermarkets and Asian grocers.

'I love the Asian influences in this dish. The crispy eschalots are fabulous with the duck.' George

Kumar's
CONFIT OCEAN TROUT
WITH ASIAN APPLE SALAD

'Kumar is a little like the tortoise and the hare,' said Peter during the 'stuffy versus fluffy' team challenge. 'He always comes out a winner, but he can be slow out of the blocks!' Kumar's deliciously light confit ocean trout was a triumph at the corporate lunch, but the dishes came out late, the main course was too heavy and crucial votes were lost.

1.25L extra virgin olive oil
1 lemon, zest cut into strips, juiced
6 sprigs lemon thyme
4 cloves garlic, bruised
1 bay leaf
4 x 220g ocean trout fillets,* pin-boned, skinned
1 tbs black or white sesame seeds
1 piece nori,* thinly shredded

DRESSING
2 cloves garlic, thinly sliced
4cm piece ginger, cut into julienne
2 tbs brown sugar
2 tbs soy sauce
2 tbs sake*
1 tbs mirin*
80ml (1/3 cup) olive oil
1 tsp sesame oil

1 lime, juiced
SALAD
1 large bulb fennel, trimmed, cut into julienne, fronds reserved
2 granny smith apples, cored, cut into julienne

1 **To make dressing,** place garlic, ginger, sugar, soy sauce, sake and mirin in a saucepan. Bring to the boil over high heat, stirring to dissolve sugar. Cool for 30 minutes, then strain into a bowl. Whisk in oils and lime juice and refrigerate until needed.

2 **To make confit trout,** place oil, zest, lemon thyme, garlic and bay leaf in a large frying pan, then attach a deep-frying thermometer to side of pan. Heat over low heat until oil temperature reaches 65°C (or when small bubbles rise from base of pan). Submerge trout in oil and cook for 3 minutes. Turn over with a spatula and cook for a further 3 minutes for medium–rare (or 5 minutes to cook through). Remove trout and drain on paper towel.

3 **To make salad,** toss together fennel, fennel fronds, apple and one-third of the dressing in a bowl and season.

4 Serve trout and salad drizzled with remaining dressing and scattered with sesame seeds and nori.

TIP Alternatively, **use salmon** instead of the trout. **Nori,** from supermarkets and Asian food shops, are sheets of seaweed. **Sake** is a Japanese rice wine from bottle shops. **Mirin** is a sweet Japanese rice wine from supermarkets.

Mat's
PEKING DUCK SPRING ROLLS

In the 'stuffy versus fluffy' challenge the red team, captained by Ellie, catered a 21st birthday party for 50 people. The birthday boy and girl and their guests loved Mat's spring rolls with spicy dipping sauce. 'Full marks for flavour,' was Matt Preston's verdict.

1.6 kg duck
1¹/₂ tbs vegetable oil
60ml (¹/₄ cup) hoisin sauce
³/₄ tsp Chinese five-spice
4 eschalots, finely chopped
6 spring onions, thinly sliced
2 cloves garlic, crushed
2 long red chillies, seeded, finely chopped

¹/₂ Chinese cabbage (wombok), very finely shredded
2 tbs Chinese rice wine (shaoxing)
80g (1 cup) bean sprouts
¹/₄ cup chopped coriander
¹/₄ tsp sesame oil
18 sheets spring roll pastry, thawed

Vegetable oil, to deep-fry
DIPPING SAUCE
80ml (¹/₃ cup) fish sauce
75g (¹/₃ cup) sugar
125ml (¹/₂ cup) lime juice
2 red chillies, seeded, finely chopped
¹/₄ cup chopped coriander leaves

1 Preheat oven to 200°C. Use poultry shears to cut down either side of the duck backbone and discard. Open duck out flat, then cut through breast to halve. Trim off excess fat and score skin on duck breast to help render fat. Combine 2 tsp of the oil, 1 tbs hoisin sauce and a pinch of Chinese five-spice and brush over duck.

2 Place duck on a rack in a large roasting pan and roast for 30 minutes or until juices run clear when a skewer is inserted into breast. Set aside until cool enough to handle, then shred meat.

3 Heat remaining oil in a large wok and cook eschalots, spring onion, garlic and chillies for 1 minute or until soft. Add cabbage and stir-fry for 2 minutes or until just wilted. Add remaining Chinese five-spice and wine and stir-fry for 1 minute or until liquid has reduced.

4 Add bean sprouts, coriander, remaining hoisin sauce and sesame oil to wok and toss together. Transfer to a bowl to cool.

5 Separate pastry sheets and lay out on work surface. Place 2 tbs filling at one end of each sheet. Fold in sides and roll up to enclose filling. Lightly brush edge with water and press to seal.

6 **To make dipping sauce,** stir fish sauce, sugar and 2 tbs water in a small saucepan over low heat until sugar has dissolved, then increase heat to medium and bring to the boil. Cook for 2 minutes, then transfer to a bowl to cool. Stir in lime juice, chillies and coriander.

7 Fill a deep-fryer or large saucepan one-third full with vegetable oil and heat over medium heat to 180°C (see cooking notes, page 264). Deep-fry spring rolls in 6 batches for 1 minute each batch or until crisp and golden. Drain on paper towel and serve with dipping sauce.

TIP Frozen spring roll pastry is available at most supermarkets.

Serves **4**
Preparation **35 minutes**
Cooking **35 minutes**

Billy's PANCETTA-WRAPPED CHICKEN WITH APPLE & CARROT

Although Billy had just seven ingredients to cook with after the blindfold taste test, the judges loved this dish and it took him into the Final 10. 'I can see this sitting on the menu in any number of good restaurants,' said Matt Preston.

4 x 220g chicken thigh or breast fillets
1½ tbs lemon thyme leaves
4 cloves garlic, crushed
125ml (½ cup) olive oil
12 slices round pancetta*
1 bunch baby (Dutch) carrots, trimmed
50g butter
1 large carrot, cut into 1cm pieces
2 small granny smith apples, peeled, cored, cut into 1cm pieces
¼ cup flat-leaf parsley
¼ cup mint leaves

1 Preheat oven to 200°C. Place chicken, lemon thyme, half the garlic and 2 tbs oil in a large bowl. Season with salt and pepper and toss to coat chicken. Place 3 pancetta slices, overlapping slightly, on a work surface. Place 1 chicken thigh lengthwise at one end of pancetta and roll up tightly to enclose. Repeat with remaining chicken and pancetta.
2 Heat 2 tbs oil in a large frying pan over high heat and cook chicken rolls, seam-side-down, for 2 minutes or until browned all over, turning often. Transfer to one end of a roasting pan and roast for 5 minutes. Wipe frying pan clean.
3 Place baby carrots and remaining 2 tbs oil in a bowl, season and toss to coat. Put carrots in other end of roasting pan. Roast with chicken rolls for a further 25 minutes or until chicken is cooked through and carrots are tender.
4 Meanwhile, heat butter in frying pan over medium-high heat and cook carrot, apples and remaining garlic, stirring occasionally, for 10 minutes or until carrot is starting to brown and apples are soft. Using a slotted spoon, transfer apple mixture to a bowl, keeping the browned butter, and combine with parsley and mint.
5 Slice chicken rolls and serve with apple mixture and carrots. Drizzle with browned butter.

TIP **Round pancetta** is available from the deli section of supermarkets. Substitute 8 slices prosciutto or bacon.

'This is a wow of a dish; one of the best things you've cooked in the competition.' Matt Preston

YES, CHEF!

Ten are left and the stakes are high. The week begins sweetly with a pudding invention test. Kate steams up a storm, but it's Dani who wins immunity. Billy goes home, then comes back, and Mat goes home instead. Marco Pierre White lulls the French and English teams into a false sense of security... and then the shouting begins! Kate's apple pie sends Peter home.

FILMING DIARY

Sunday

EPISODE 55 Are you in a pudding kind of mood? Gary is, and he's getting hungry.

Monday

EPISODE 56 Billy's elimination guinea fowl in a salt crust sends him packing.

Tuesday

EPISODE 57 Dani matches Alessandro Pavoni point for point and wins immunity.

Wednesday

EPISODE 58 The Marco Pierre White experience leaves the blue team reeling.

Thursday

EPISODE 59 Peter loses to Kate's apple pie in a 'techniques' elimination test.

Friday

EPISODE 60 MasterChef all-stars Andre, Jimmy and Alvin are back for masterclass.

Week 10

THE PROOF'S IN THE PUDDING

Gary cleverly deduces that Hayden has never eaten a steamed pudding in his life: 'You see? That is a surfer's stomach. *This* is a pudding stomach!' The Top 10's first challenge is to cook a pudding in one hour. With 10 seconds to go, Peter's pudding is still molten and Gary is in teasing mood: 'How are you going to get the soup on the plate, Peter?'

Kate is victorious with her 'spectacular' white chocolate and raspberry pudding. 'Yeah, this is rubbish,' says Gary, trying to scrape more from the empty plate. Kate chooses figs for the Middle Eastern invention test. Mat unpacks his basket to find he's forgotten the figs; but Billy's forgotten the butter and some Middle Eastern bartering makes everyone happy. 'Don't forget: we want a figalicious dish,' announces George, to groans.

Dani's frozen baklava is the star of the

Below: Dani's brilliant 'rock and roll' frozen baklava sees her cooking a cuttlefish chequerboard in a 'grudge match' against Ormeggio's Alessandro Pavoni. But Alessandro is a born teacher and can't resist giving Dani a helping hand.

Captain Dani gets to choose cuisine – French or English? – and her 'dream team' of Kate, Hayden, Peter and Michael to cook a three-course lunch at Felix. Alana will captain the red 'English underdogs'.

The teams are starstruck to find Marco Pierre White at the restaurant. 'I'm here to guide you, assist you and protect you,' says kindly father-figure Marco.

'Are you happy, or terrified?' Gary asks the contestants. 'Both,' they all murmur.

Alana makes motivational cards for her team: 'Speed' for Sun; 'Confidence' for Billy, and 'Be clean!' for Ellie. Dani takes her whole team off main courses and the blues start to fall apart. When service begins, Marco flips a switch from gentle father-figure to world-famous chef. 'Shout at me like I shout at you!' he yells – when he's not yelling at Peter to get his quails cooked. Hayden's bisque is a triumph, but so is Billy's pork belly and Alana's team of underdogs wins the day.

Clockwise from below: 'We're going to be real chefs today,' says Alana, captain of the 'English' team; Gary loves every minute of the challenge, even the shouting: 'I stood at the pass, thinking "Ooh, I wish he'd tell me off, too!"'; Marco Pierre White is impressed by Billy's 'clever' pork belly.

'He'd been so quiet and gentle, like a spiritual leader. Then he turned psycho.' Peter

day, while fig fiascos send Billy, Hayden and Mat to elimination, cooking guinea fowl in a salt crust. Billy's heading home, but Hayden tries to view the experience positively: 'It's good to know that, if I'm ever going to cook a salt-encrusted fowl again, I'll do it right!'

Alessandro Pavoni is back in the kitchen for a 'grudge match'. It might be a matter of chef's honour, but Alessandro has a 'huge heart and wants to see me succeed,' says Dani. The chef helps her plate up and then pins an immunity pin to her jacket.

MARCO PIERRE BITES
Bad news for Mat is good news for Billy, who's back after a surprise visit from Matt Preston. Mat, a true Gen Y tech-head, is going home for using his mobile phone.

Kate's
RASPBERRY & WHITE CHOCOLATE
PUDDINGS WITH KAHLUA ICE-CREAM

KAHLUA ICE-CREAM
125ml (½ cup) pouring cream
125ml (½ cup) milk
2 egg yolks
110g (½ cup) caster sugar
30ml kahlua
WHITE CHOCOLATE SHARDS
50g white chocolate, melted

RASPBERRY SAUCE
110g (½ cup) caster sugar
125g raspberries, plus extra,
  to serve
3 tsp lemon juice
PUDDINGS
125g unsalted butter, softened
60g caster sugar

1 tsp vanilla extract
2 eggs, separated
100g white chocolate,
  finely grated
75g (½ cup) plain flour
1 tsp baking powder
2 tbs milk

1 To make kahlua ice-cream, heat cream and milk over medium heat until almost at boiling point. Whisk egg yolks and sugar in a bowl until pale. Whisking continuously, pour hot cream mixture onto yolk mixture in a slow stream. Strain mixture into a clean saucepan and stir over low heat for 7 minutes or until thick enough to coat the back of a wooden spoon. Transfer to a bowl and leave for 10 minutes, stirring occasionally to release the heat. Stir in kahlua, cover with plastic wrap and refrigerate for 3 hours or until well chilled. Churn in an ice-cream machine until frozen. Transfer to an airtight container and freeze for 4 hours or until firm.

2 To make white chocolate shards, line an oven tray with baking paper. Spread white chocolate thinly over paper and refrigerate for 15 minutes or until set. Break into shards and keep cool.

3 To make raspberry sauce, stir sugar and 125ml (½ cup) water in a saucepan over low heat without boiling until sugar dissolves. Increase heat and bring to the boil. Cook for 1 minute, then remove from heat and add one-third of the raspberries, crushing gently with a wooden spoon. Leave until cool to let raspberries infuse. Press through a fine sieve, discarding solids. Process syrup in a food processor with half the remaining raspberries until smooth. Add lemon juice and then strain again.

4 To make puddings, grease six 125ml (½-cup) dariole moulds. Using an electric mixer, beat butter, sugar and vanilla in a small bowl of an electric mixer until pale and fluffy. Add egg yolks, one at a time, beating well after each addition. Stir in grated chocolate.

5 Sift flour and baking powder twice. Add to chocolate mixture with milk and gently fold to combine. Beat egg whites to firm peaks. Fold a large spoonful of egg white into batter to loosen mixture, then gently fold in remaining mixture with a metal spoon until just combined.

6 Spoon 1 tbs raspberry sauce into each mould. Divide half the batter among the moulds, and place 2 raspberries in each mould. Spoon in remaining batter and smooth surface. Cut a 40cm piece of foil and grease one side with butter. Place a 40cm piece of baking paper on the greased foil and press together. Cut into 6 equal pieces. Fold a 2cm pleat in centre of each. Place, paper-side-down, over puddings and tie securely with kitchen string or rubber bands.

7 Place moulds in a large saucepan. Pour in enough boiling water to come halfway up the moulds. Cover pan, bring water back to the boil, then reduce heat and cook at high simmer for 20 minutes or until puddings are cooked through. Cool puddings slightly, then turn out onto plates and serve with ice-cream, fresh raspberries, sauce and chocolate shards.

'This is spectacular!' George

Sun's
SPICED PUDDINGS WITH APPLE, RHUBARB & BUTTERSCOTCH SAUCE

The judges were looking for a classic steamed pudding 'like Nanna used to make', but updated for the 21st century. For Sun this was a completely new challenge: she'd never made a steamed pudding before. Matt Preston loved the 'beautifully complimentary flavours of rich butterscotch and sharp ginger' in this dish.

SPICED PUDDINGS
150g (1 cup) self-raising flour
1/2 tsp baking powder
1 tsp ground cinnamon
1/2 tsp ground cloves
125g softened unsalted butter
125g caster sugar
2 tbs maple syrup
1 tbs brandy
2 eggs

CARAMELISED APPLE
55g (1/4 cup) caster sugar
2 granny smith apples, peeled, quartered, cored, sliced
20g butter
STEWED RHUBARB
55g (1/4 cup) caster sugar
4 stalks rhubarb, cut into 1cm slices
1/2 tsp lemon juice

APPLE MASCARPONE
1 granny smith apple, peeled
2 tbs icing sugar
1/4 tsp vanilla bean paste
125g mascarpone
BUTTERSCOTCH SAUCE
70g butter
110g (1/2 firmly packed cup) brown sugar
50g mascarpone

1 **To make puddings,** preheat oven to 180°C. Grease six 125ml (1/2-cup) dariole moulds.
2 Sift flour, baking powder and spices twice. Using an electric mixer, beat butter, sugar and maple syrup until light and fluffy. Beat in brandy. Add eggs, one at a time, beating well after each. Add spiced flour and mix well. Spoon batter into moulds and smooth surface.
3 Cut a 40cm piece of foil and grease one side with butter. Place a 40cm piece of baking paper on the greased foil and press together. Cut into 6 equal pieces. Fold a 2cm pleat in centre of each. Place, paper-side-down, over puddings and tie securely with kitchen string or rubber bands. Place moulds in a large roasting pan. Pour in enough boiling water to come halfway up the moulds. Bake for 30 minutes or until puddings are cooked through. Cool slightly.
4 **To make caramelised apples,** place sugar and 2 tbs water in a frying pan. Stir over low heat until sugar dissolves, then bring to the boil. Cook without stirring for 6 minutes or until lightly golden. Add apple and butter and cook, turning occasionally, for 5 minutes or until softened.
5 **To make stewed rhubarb,** place sugar and 2 tbs water in a small saucepan over medium heat and stir until sugar has dissolved. Bring to the boil and stir in rhubarb and lemon juice. Reduce heat to low and simmer for 5 minutes or until rhubarb is soft.
6 **To make apple mascarpone,** grate apple, place in a muslin cloth and squeeze juices into a bowl. Beat sugar and vanilla into mascarpone until smooth. Gradually add 60ml (1/4 cup) of the apple juice and mix well. Refrigerate until required.
7 **To make butterscotch sauce,** melt butter in a saucepan over low heat, add brown sugar and stir until dissolved. Bring to a simmer and cook, stirring continuously, for 3 minutes until combined, then simmer, without stirring, for 2 minutes. Remove from heat and whisk in mascarpone.
8 Turn out puddings and top with apple and rhubarb. Serve with apple mascarpone and sauce.

Dani's
FIG & PISTACHIO FROZEN BAKLAVA

4 figs, halved
Roasted chopped pistachios,
  pistachio fairy floss* and
  pomegranate seeds, to serve
ICE-CREAM
375ml (1½ cups) milk
250ml (1 cup) pouring cream
1 cinnamon quill, broken
2 cardamom pods, bruised
1 tbs honey
1 tbs finely grated orange zest
1 vanilla bean, split, seeds
  scraped

½ tsp mixed spice
150g (⅔ cup) caster sugar,
  plus 1 tsp, extra
7 egg yolks
5 figs, chopped
35g (¼ cup) pistachios, roasted,
  coarsely ground
PASTRY
6 sheets filo pastry
80g unsalted butter, melted
120g (1 cup) ground almonds
35g (¼ cup) pistachios, roasted,
  ground

SYRUP
3 oranges, juiced
1 lemon, juiced
165g (¾ cup) caster sugar
1 tbs rosewater
3 tsp honey
2 cardamom pods, bruised
1 tsp ground cinnamon

1 **To make ice-cream,** combine milk, cream, cinnamon quill, cardamom pods, honey, orange zest, vanilla bean and seeds, mixed spice and half the sugar in a saucepan and heat until almost boiling. Turn off heat and leave for 5 minutes to infuse.

2 Whisk remaining sugar and egg yolks until thick and pale. Gradually whisk in hot milk mixture. Return to saucepan and stir over low heat without boiling for 6 minutes or until mixture thickens enough to coat the back of a wooden spoon. Strain into a clean bowl and leave for 10 minutes, stirring occasionally to release heat. Cover with plastic and chill for 3 hours.

3 Process half the figs with the 1 tsp sugar until almost smooth and stir into custard. Churn in an ice-cream machine until frozen. Line two 20 x 30cm slice pans with plastic wrap, letting it overhang the long sides. Fold remaining chopped figs and pistachios through the ice-cream. Spread into pans, cover with plastic wrap and freeze for 3 hours or until firm.

4 **To make pastry,** preheat oven to 150°C and line 3 oven trays with baking paper. Place 1 sheet of filo in each tray and brush half the sheet with melted butter. Sprinkle this half with 2 tbs ground almonds and 2 tsp pistachios, then fold the other half of the sheet over. Repeat with another sheet of pastry and place on top of first – you will have a stack on each oven tray. Cut each stack into 8 triangles (24 triangles in total). Place on trays, brush tops with melted butter and bake for 10 minutes or until crisp and golden. Cool.

5 **To make syrup,** place all ingredients in a saucepan and stir over medium heat without boiling until sugar has dissolved. Bring to the boil and cook for 10 minutes or until reduced by half.

6 Brush hot syrup over the pastry triangles and leave to cool, keeping remaining syrup.

7 **To serve,** cut ice-cream into triangles the same size as pastry triangles. Top one pastry triangle with a layer of ice-cream, place another layer of pastry on top, one more of ice-cream and a final layer of pastry. Make 8 stacks. Brush with syrup, sprinkle with chopped pistachios. Add a fig half to each plate and drizzle with syrup. Garnish with fairy floss and pomegranate seeds.

TIP **Pistachio fairy floss** is a pale green Middle Eastern-style fairy floss, available from specialist food shops.

'Rock and roll, Dani! I bags this recipe
for my restaurant.' George

Peter's
FIG & EGGPLANT BRAISE
WITH FLATBREAD & YOGHURT DRESSING

The theme of the invention test was 'Middle Eastern' and Kate chose figs as the core ingredient. After his dessert disaster that morning, Peter was determined to cook a savoury fig dish: 'I'm very happy with this... it tastes like the Middle East.' Gary agreed: 'This is a smashing dish. I want more, but it's time for me to walk away.'

1 tbs olive oil
2 onions, chopped
4 eschalots, thinly sliced
4 cloves garlic, crushed
1 tbs ground cumin
1 tbs ground coriander
1 tsp ground turmeric
2 tomatoes, chopped
1 large eggplant, cut into
   3cm pieces

400g can chickpeas, rinsed,
   drained
400g can diced tomatoes
150g button mushrooms, sliced
Pinch of saffron
1 cinnamon quill
3 figs, quartered lengthwise
FLATBREAD
6 figs, cut into 5mm slices
300g (2 cups) plain flour

70g (½ cup) roasted pistachios,
   finely chopped
Olive oil, to shallow-fry
YOGHURT DRESSING
1 Lebanese cucumber, grated
1 cup mint leaves, chopped
200g plain yoghurt
Pinch of sumac

1 Heat the olive oil in a large deep frying pan over medium heat and cook the onions, eschalots and garlic for 5 minutes or until soft and lightly golden. Add the ground spices and cook, stirring, for 1 minute or until fragrant.

2 Stir in the fresh tomatoes and cook, stirring occasionally, for 5 minutes or until broken down. Add eggplant, chickpeas, canned tomatoes and mushrooms.

3 Combine saffron with 180ml (¾ cup) warm water and add to pan with the cinnamon quill. Stir, cover and bring to the boil. Reduce heat to low and simmer, covered, for 20 minutes or until eggplant is tender. Stir in figs and cook for 10 minutes or until figs are soft. Season.

4 Meanwhile, to make flatbread, preheat the oven to 150°C and line an oven tray with baking paper. Arrange fig slices in a single layer and bake for 30 minutes or until dry and chewy. Cool.

5 Mix flour and a pinch of salt in a large bowl and make a well in the centre. Add 125ml (½ cup) water, mix with a wooden spoon and then with your hands, adding more water, if necessary, to form a soft dough. Turn out onto a lightly floured surface and knead for 3 minutes or until smooth and elastic. Wrap in plastic wrap and rest for 20 minutes.

6 Divide the dough into 6 portions and roll out each portion to 3mm thick. Arrange dried figs and sprinkle pistachios onto one half of each piece. Season and fold over to enclose filling. Roll again to flatten and seal. Heat a large frying pan over medium heat and brush lightly with oil. Cook flatbreads, one at a time, for 2 minutes on each side or until golden.

7 To make yoghurt dressing, combine the cucumber and a pinch of salt in a bowl and leave for 5 minutes. Squeeze to remove excess liquid, then mix cucumber with mint, yoghurt and sumac.

8 Serve fig and eggplant braise with flatbread and yoghurt dressing.

Serves **6**
Preparation **45 minutes**
Cooking **2½ hours**

Billy's
PORK BELLY WITH CIDER GRAVY

'Who made the pork belly?' asked Matt Moran after the Marco Pierre White challenge. Billy's pork belly forced the judges to break their self-imposed rule of 'only a little bit at tasting'. Matt Preston showed his appreciation by spilling gravy down his pristine laundered shirt. 'Thank you for coming back and giving us the best dish of the series,' said George to Billy.

PORK BELLY
1.5 kg piece pork belly
2 tbs sea salt
2 tbs olive oil
BRAISING STOCK
1.25L cider
500ml (2 cups) chicken stock
4 small carrots, peeled, trimmed
1 leek, chopped
2 onions, chopped

1 tbs fennel seeds
2 bay leaves
4 star anise
BRUSSELS SPROUTS
50g butter
1kg brussels sprouts, halved
100g rindless bacon,
 thinly sliced
CARAMELISED APPLES
125g butter

5 granny smith apples, peeled,
 quartered, cored
3g fennel pollen,* optional
CARROT PUREE
160g butter
4 carrots, grated
CIDER GRAVY
3 sprigs lemon thyme
250ml (1 cup) apple juice

1 For pork belly, preheat oven to 220°C. Use a small sharp knife or thin blade to score skin of pork belly, making cuts 3cm apart. Rub salt and oil into skin, place in a large deep roasting pan and roast for 40 minutes or until skin has crackled and blistered. Remove from pan and reduce oven to 160°C.

2 To make braising stock, combine all ingredients in a large saucepan over high heat and bring to the boil. Pour braising stock into roasting pan without straining. Return pork belly to roasting pan so meat is completely submerged but the crisp skin stays dry above the liquid. Cook for 2 hours or until very tender. Remove pork belly from pan and keep warm. Strain stock into a large saucepan and keep the braised carrots.

3 Meanwhile, for brussels sprouts, melt butter in a large frying pan over medium heat and cook sprouts and bacon for 5 minutes or until lightly browned. Transfer to a large roasting pan and roast for 30 minutes or until sprouts are tender and well browned.

4 To make caramelised apples, melt butter in a frying pan over medium heat and cook apples for 6 minutes or until soft, turning occasionally. Sprinkle with fennel pollen and set aside.

5 To make carrot purée, melt 60g butter in a frying pan and cook grated carrot over low–medium heat for 10 minutes or until tender. Transfer to a blender with reserved braised carrots. Purée, adding remaining butter a little at a time, until smooth and glossy. Season.

7 To make cider gravy, skim fat from surface of stock. Add lemon thyme and apple juice and bring to the boil over high heat. Reduce heat to medium and simmer for 30 minutes or until liquid has reduced and thickened.

8 Slice pork belly thickly and serve with carrot purée, caramelised apples, sprouts and a drizzle of cider gravy.

TIP Fennel pollen is available from specialist spice shops such as Herbie's Spices in Sydney (herbies.com.au).

Serves **6**
Preparation **45 minutes + 2 hours chilling**
Cooking **1 hour 40 minutes**

Hayden's
LOBSTER BISQUE WITH SCALLOPS

1.5kg live lobster
60ml (¼ cup) olive oil
60ml (¼ cup) cognac
3 cloves garlic, peeled, sliced
2 stalks celery, chopped
2 carrots, chopped
2 onions, chopped
1 leek, chopped
500ml (2 cups) white wine

2 bay leaves
400g can diced tomatoes
2 tbs tomato paste
½ tsp cayenne pepper
125ml (½ cup) pouring cream
35g (¼ cup) plain flour
60g butter
12 scallops, without roe
Caviar and micro herbs, to serve

COURT BOUILLON
250ml (1 cup) white wine
1 leek, chopped
1 carrot, chopped
1 onion, chopped
1 stalk celery, chopped
8 black peppercorns
2 bay leaves

1 Place lobster in the freezer for 2 hours to stun it. Wear rubber gloves or protect hands with a folded tea towel. Place lobster on a large board; put one hand on the head and other on the tail and twist tail and body in different directions to separate. Set tail aside and use a heavy cleaver to chop head in half lengthwise. Scoop out and keep the tomalley (soft mustard-coloured substance). Chop head and legs into rough pieces, discarding the antennae.

2 To make court bouillon, combine all ingredients with 2.25L water in a large saucepan. Bring to the boil, reduce heat and simmer for 20 minutes. Thread a skewer lengthwise through the lobster tail to keep it straight while cooking. Lower lobster tail into the bouillon and cook gently for 8 minutes or until just cooked through. Plunge into a bowl of iced water to stop cooking. Strain the court bouillon, keeping 2L liquid. Cut down the underside of the lobster shell with kitchen scissors and remove shell. Slice lobster into 6 medallions.

3 Heat 2 tbs olive oil in a large frying pan. Add chopped lobster and cook over medium–high heat for 4 minutes or until shell turns deep red. Add cognac and flambé. Transfer to a bowl.

4 Heat remaining oil in the frying pan over medium heat and cook garlic and vegetables for 10 minutes or until very soft and just lightly coloured. Return lobster shell to pan. Add white wine and bay leaves and cook for 8 minutes or until reduced by half.

5 Add diced tomatoes, tomato paste, cayenne pepper and 2L court bouillon. Bring to the boil over low heat and simmer for 45 minutes or until thickened and reduced slightly, mashing occasionally with a potato masher to break up lobster and release the flavours.

6 Preheat oven to 150°C. Wrap lobster medallions in foil and reheat in the oven for 10 minutes. Strain bisque through a coarse sieve, pressing down on solids with a ladle to release flavours. Discard solids and strain bisque again through a fine sieve. Pour bisque into a clean saucepan and bring to the boil over medium heat. Season with salt and pepper; add the cream and the reserved tomalley. Mix flour and butter in a small bowl and slowly whisk small pieces into the bisque. Simmer for 2 minutes or until thickened.

7 Heat 1 tbs olive oil in a large frying pan over high heat and cook scallops in 2 batches for 1 minute each side or until just cooked. Season.

8 To serve, ladle bisque into bowls. Add 2 scallops and a lobster medallion to each bowl and top with caviar and micro herbs.

'That's the best bisque you've ever made, isn't it?' Marco Pierre White to Hayden

Serves **8**
Preparation **30 minutes + 1 hour chilling**
Cooking **55 minutes**

Kate's
APPLE PIE WITH VANILLA CUSTARD

The blue 'French' team headed to a 'techniques' elimination test. In the final round, the judges were looking for 'beautiful, buttery, crumbly pastry and velvety, creamy custard'. Kate knew exactly what she was doing, but so did Peter and the judges struggled to decide between them. This light-as-a-feather pie and restaurant-quality custard kept Kate safe.

PASTRY
300g (2 cups) plain flour
200g unsalted butter, chopped
80g (1/3 cup) crème fraîche
FILLING
1.2kg granny smith apples,
    peeled, cored, cut into
    3cm chunks

110g (1/2 cup) caster sugar
1/2 vanilla bean, split, seeds
    scraped
40g (1/4 cup) blanched almonds,
    roasted,* chopped
1 egg, lightly beaten
2 tsp demerara sugar

VANILLA CUSTARD
180ml (3/4 cup) milk
180ml (3/4 cup) pouring cream
1 vanilla bean, split, seeds
    scraped
3 egg yolks
55g (1/4 cup) caster sugar

1 To make pastry, process flour and butter in a food processor until mixture resembles crumbs. Add crème fraîche and process until mixture just comes together. Divide into 2 portions, one slightly larger than the other, and shape into 2 discs. Wrap in plastic and chill for 30 minutes.

2 To make filling, put apples and sugar in a saucepan with 250ml (1 cup) water. Add vanilla bean and seeds. Bring to the boil, reduce heat to low–medium and simmer for 5 minutes or until apples are tender but still hold their shape. Drain and cool. Discard vanilla bean.

3 Preheat oven to 180°C. Roll out larger pastry disc on a sheet of baking paper to fit a 23cm tart pan with a removable base. Line pan with pastry and trim edge. Line with a sheet of baking paper and fill with dried rice or beans; refrigerate for 30 minutes. Bake for 10 minutes, then remove paper and rice and bake for a further 10 minutes or until lightly golden. Cool.

4 Sprinkle almonds over pastry base and fill with apple. Roll out remaining pastry and place over pie. Press gently around edge of pan to trim off overhanging pastry. Brush pastry with egg and sprinkle with sugar. Bake for 30 minutes or until golden.

5 To make vanilla custard, combine milk, cream, vanilla bean and seeds in a small saucepan over gentle heat. Heat almost to boiling point, then remove from heat. Whisk yolks and sugar until pale, then slowly pour in the hot milk, whisking to combine. Discard vanilla bean. Pour custard back into a clean saucepan, place over low heat and stir with a wooden spoon without boiling for 7 minutes or until custard thickens enough to coat back of the spoon. Strain into a jug.

6 Serve apple pie warm or at room temperature with custard.

TIP **To roast nuts,** spread over an oven tray and bake at 180°C for 5 minutes.

NEW YORK STORIES

The Top 8 find themselves in the city that never sleeps. Michael enjoys some food theatre and Dani's in tears, while Sun's 'art-gallery' cake sends her to her room. Michael gets to play a game of strategy at the United Nations. Ellie defeats a Tuscan lion in Central Park, and then races to victory with Alana. Billy becomes a soul brother, but Sun's soul food eliminates her.

FILMING DIARY

Sunday

EPISODE 61 The Top 8 explore New York and Michael captures the spirit of the city.

Monday

EPISODE 62 MIchael is strategic at the United Nations, leaving Billy in strife.

Tuesday

EPISODE 63 Ellie finally makes her mark – in Central Park – and wins immunity.

Wednesday

EPISODE 64 It's a race to find the recipe and cook for the ultimate dinner party.

Thursday

EPISODE 65 Sun's Harlem soul food turns out to be soul destroying.

Friday

EPISODE 66 Michael and Alana enjoy a masterclass tour of NY culinary hotspots.

Week 11

IF YOU CAN MAKE IT THERE...

'Welcome to New York. Welcome to the time of your life,' says Matt P, in front of the Statue of Liberty. The Top 8 have three hours to explore a corner of the city and transform its heart into a dish.

In Brooklyn Dani becomes a 'soda jerk' and makes an old-fashioned egg cream. On the Lower East Side Sun is distracted by her passion for the stark New Museum of Contemporary Art. She decides to stack a honey cake in the same shape... she's never tasted the cake but a lady in Katz's Deli likes the recipe a lot.

It's time to hit the kitchen: Dani's whoopie pies burn; Sun's cake crumbles under her knife, and the huffing and puffing gets ever louder. But Michael's having a great time. He puts on a vendor's cap to serve the judges his 'food cart' 43rd Street taco and George insists on handing over a dollar – the first time Michael's ever been paid to cook.

Below: Dani explores Brooklyn to learn about soda jerks and whoopie pies, while Sun is sent to the delis of the Lower East Side and decides to cook a cake she's never tasted.

'There's something in the water here that agrees with me!' Ellie

ELLIE TAKES ON THE BIG APPLE

Ellie's surprise UN win (well, surprise for Michael) sees her cooking for immunity against Cesare Casella of New York's Salumeria Rosi. She takes on the 'Tuscan lion' – who turns out to be rather more of an Italian pussycat – and beats him at his own pasta to win an immunity pin.

The 'ultimate dinner party' challenge starts in Times Square with a race to find a recipe. After a dreadful start, Alana and Ellie cook an almost-perfect gold bar dessert from Corton. Kate and Michael make David Chang's steak and chips, and are so surprised to find they're not in elimination that they both burst into tears.

Dani and Hayden have to cook ribs and fried chicken in Harlem with Billy and Sun. There's friction at the fryers, not a lot of 'love' in the air, and Sun's heading home.

Clockwise from below: The judges surprise the Top 8 in Times Square; Hayden cooks up a great dessert at the United Nations; Chef Cesare Casella, the 'Tuscan lion', turns out to be a 'truly hospitable' Italian, who serves Ellie a cocktail during their Central Park immunity challenge.

'This could be the most embarrassing moment ever,' says Dani, who's presenting 'cupcakes and milk' to the judges. Her milk soda and bubbly bit of 'theatre' save her, but for Sun the fun stops today. She's put into lockdown in her hotel room in the middle of the world's most exciting city.

MICHAEL'S GAME OF STRATEGY

'Holey moley, guacamole!' says Billy, as the contestants arrive at the United Nations building. Michael's black envelope gives him unprecedented power: to choose who cooks which canapé. He plays it cleverly: best mate Hayden gets a dish 'to make him look good'; Kate's wrestling a tuna 'bigger than my children'; Dani makes 'chocolate lollipops' because 'he knows I'm awful with a piping bag' and Billy's cold soup is never going to win votes.

Michael's
43RD STREET TACO

2 x 250g scotch fillet steaks
1 tbs olive oil
500g beef chuck steak, cut into
    4cm pieces
1 onion, roughly chopped
2 cloves garlic, roughly chopped
400g can diced tomatoes
120g (1/2 cup) sour cream
1/2 lime, juiced
24 small tortillas, warmed
MEXICAN CHILLI PASTE
6 (25g) dried chipotle chillies*
2 (20g) dried ancho chillies*
2 tbs cumin seeds

2 tbs coriander seeds
3 cloves
1 cinnamon quill
1 tsp smoked paprika
1 long green chilli, chopped
1 lime, juiced
60ml (1/4 cup) olive oil
TOMATO SALSA
2 tomatoes, seeded, diced
1/2 red onion, diced
1 small jalapeño chilli,* finely
    chopped
1/2 cup coriander, finely chopped
1 lime, juiced

STREET NUTS
45g (1/3 cup) slivered almonds
50g (1/3 cup) sunflower seeds
1/4 tsp cumin seeds
1/4 tsp coriander seeds
2 tsp caster sugar
CORN & BLACK BEAN SALAD
1 tbs olive oil
2 cobs corn, kernels removed
400g can black beans,* rinsed
1 lime, juiced
1/2 cup coriander leaves, chopped

1 To make chilli paste, soak dried chillies in 250ml (1 cup) boiling water for 20 minutes or until soft. Dry-fry whole spices over medium heat for 2 minutes or until fragrant, tossing often. Cool. Drain chillies, keeping liquid, and remove seeds. Grind toasted spices to a fine powder. Add soaked chillies, paprika, green chilli, lime juice, oil and 1/2 tsp salt. Process to a smooth paste.

2 Marinate scotch fillet in 1/2 cup chilli paste in a bowl. Cover and refrigerate until needed.

3 Heat oil in a saucepan over high heat and cook chuck steak, turning often, for 5 minutes or until browned. Lift out and set aside. Reduce heat to medium and cook onion and garlic for 5 minutes or until soft and golden. Add remaining chilli paste and cook, stirring, for 1 minute or until fragrant. Return chuck to pan with tomatoes, chilli soaking liquid and 250ml (1 cup) water. Stir, bring to the boil, then reduce heat to low–medium and cook, covered, for 1 hour. Uncover and cook, stirring occasionally, for 30 minutes or until sauce is thick and meat is very tender. Shred meat in pan with forks and cover to keep warm.

4 Meanwhile, to make tomato salsa, combine all ingredients in a bowl and season with salt.

5 For street nuts, dry-fry nuts and seeds over medium heat for 4 minutes, tossing often. Add sugar, season and cook, stirring, for 1 minute or until sugar is caramelised. Transfer to a bowl.

6 Heat a greased chargrill pan over medium–high heat. Cook fillet steaks for 4 minutes each side for medium–rare or until cooked to your liking. Rest for 5 minutes, then thinly slice.

7 To make salad, heat oil in a frying pan over medium heat and cook corn and beans, stirring often, for 3 minutes or until corn is tender. Stir in lime juice and coriander and season.

8 Mix sour cream with lime juice. Place a little shredded meat, sliced steak and corn salad on each tortilla, scatter with tomato salsa and street nuts and top with sour cream.

TIP **Chipotle and ancho** are common names for dried jalapeño and poblano chillies. Buy at specialist shops or online at Herbie's Spices (herbies.com.au). **Jalapeño chillies** are from supermarkets. Use 1 long green chilli or 1 tbs pickled jalapeño chillies, available in jars from supermarkets. **You can substitute kidney beans** for black beans.

Serves **4**
Preparation **30 minutes**
Cooking **3 hours 10 minutes**

Billy's
NEW YORK OSSO BUCO

Billy was inspired by the Bronx, New York's 'little Italy', where *The Godfather* was filmed. 'I'm going to just rock it and risk it! I want fun on my plate.' He served a starter with 'pepper spray' and graffiti on the plate, and Godfather-style capsicum 'blood splatters' around his osso buco. The sherry and capsicum give this osso buco a flavour of Spain, rather than Italy.

1kg veal osso buco
2 tbs olive oil
1 onion, chopped
3 cloves garlic, chopped
3 tomatoes, chopped
1L (4 cups) beef stock
250ml (1 cup) Pedro Ximénez
    amontillado sherry

3 sprigs thyme
3 sprigs oregano
150g roasted red capsicum
2 cooked artichokes, halved
2 tbs capers, drained
Olive oil, to shallow-fry
MASH
500g rock salt

3 x 250g sebago or desiree
    potatoes, unpeeled, washed
75g butter, chopped
WILTED ROCKET
1 tbs olive oil
2 cloves garlic, chopped
2 bunches rocket, trimmed

1 Season osso buco with salt and pepper. Heat oil in a large heavy-based pan over medium–high heat and cook the meat in 2 batches for 2 minutes each side or until well browned. Set aside.

2 Add onion to pan and cook over medium heat for 5 minutes or until soft. Add garlic and cook for 1 minute. Stir in tomatoes, scraping bottom of pan. Add stock, sherry, thyme and oregano.

3 Return osso buco to pan, making sure it's covered with sauce (add water, if needed). Cover and bring to the boil. Reduce heat to low and simmer for 2½ hours or until tender. Uncover, remove meat with a slotted spoon, then increase heat to medium–high. Cook for 20 minutes or until sauce has reduced and thickened, then return meat to heat through.

4 **Meanwhile, to make mash,** preheat oven to 200°C. Spread rock salt in a thick layer onto an oven tray. Place potatoes on salt and prick all over. Bake for 1½ hours or until soft when tested with a skewer. Cut in half and scoop out potato. Press through a sieve or ricer and mash well. Beat in butter and season with salt and pepper.

5 **To make wilted rocket,** heat oil in a frying pan over medium–high heat and cook garlic for 30 seconds. Add rocket and toss until wilted. Keep warm.

6 Process the red capsicum until smooth. Season.

7 Heat a frying pan or grill pan over medium–high heat. Cook artichokes, cut-side-down, for 1 minute or until caramelised.

8 Dry capers thoroughly with paper towel. Heat 2cm oil in a small frying pan over medium–high heat and cook capers for 2 minutes or until crisp. Drain on paper towels.

9 Serve osso buco with capsicum purée, wilted rocket, mash and artichoke. Sprinkle with capers.

Alana's
SMOKED LAMB RACKS WITH HONEY-THYME CUSTARD & CUCUMBER ESSENCE

Alana wanted to create a dish that was inspired by the Greek community of New York's Astoria, but could easily be served in upmarket Park Avenue. She combined the smokiness and vibrancy of Astoria with the flavours of Greece: honey and thyme.

110g (½ firmly packed cup) brown sugar
100g long-grain rice
40g (½ cup) black tea leaves
2 tsp dried oregano
3 bay leaves
2 tbs honey
1 tsp ground cumin
20g butter, melted
4 x 3-cutlet lamb racks, Frenched*

Breadcrumbs, toasted
Flaked toasted almonds and thyme, to serve
HONEY-THYME CUSTARD
10g butter
2 cloves garlic, chopped
200ml milk
200ml pouring cream
2 sprigs thyme
2 tbs honey

3 egg yolks
1 egg
CUCUMBER ESSENCE
3 Lebanese cucumbers
¼ cup parsley, roughly chopped
¼ cup mint leaves, roughly chopped
1 tbs lemon juice

1 **To make honey-thyme custard,** melt butter in a small saucepan over low–medium heat. Add garlic and cook, stirring, for 1 minute or until soft and fragrant but not coloured. Add milk, cream, thyme and honey. Season with salt and white pepper and bring just to the boil.
2 Whisk the egg yolks and egg in a bowl. Gradually pour in the hot milk mixture, whisking continuously. Strain through a fine sieve and pour into 4 lightly oiled 125ml (½-cup) ramekins.
3 Cover each ramekin tightly with plastic wrap. Place in a steamer over a saucepan of simmering water and cook, covered, for 10 minutes or until just set. Remove from pan.
4 Line a wok with 2 sheets of foil. Combine sugar, rice, tea, oregano and bay leaves and spread onto foil. Heat over high heat for 5 minutes or until mixture begins to smoke. Reduce heat to medium. Meanwhile, combine honey, cumin and butter and season with salt and pepper. Toss lamb in honey mixture to coat. Place a lightly oiled rack in the wok and arrange lamb on rack. Cover wok and smoke the meat for 15 minutes, turning every 5 minutes. Transfer meat to a plate, cover loosely with foil and leave to rest for 5 minutes.
5 **To make cucumber essence,** roughly chop 2½ cucumbers and finely dice the remainder. Process the chopped cucumber, herbs and lemon juice in a food processor until smooth. Add 60ml (¼ cup) iced water and process briefly to mix. Strain through a muslin-lined sieve.
6 Divide lamb racks among plates, scatter with breadcrumbs, diced cucumber, flaked almonds and thyme and serve with honey-thyme custard and cucumber essence.

TIP **To French** a bone is to scrape away all the meat and fat for presentation. See cooking notes page 264.

'The smokiness of the lamb with that thyme custard is really beautiful.' Matt Preston

Serves **6 as a starter**
Preparation **50 minutes**
Cooking **20 minutes**

Ellie's
DRY-AGED BEEF WITH TOMATO RAVIOLI

Ellie loved her time in New York: 'I think we should finish the rest of the competition here!' For her first New York challenge, she explored the groovy Meatpacking District: the cobblestoned streets are home to high-fashion outlets set among the traditional butchers. Ellie's playful dish combined deliciously marinated beef with contemporary ravioli.

2 tbs olive oil
2 slices prosciutto, chopped
35g (½ cup) fresh breadcrumbs
1 green chilli, seeded, chopped
1 tbs finely chopped mint
1 tbs finely chopped basil
2 cloves garlic, crushed
1 tbs olive oil
2 x 300g dry-aged New York
  steaks*

TOMATO RAVIOLI
1 tbs olive oil
½ red onion, finely chopped
2 cloves garlic, crushed
12 cherry tomatoes
12 gow gee wrappers
CORIANDER PESTO
½ cup coriander leaves
2 tsp sesame seeds, toasted
½ lemon, zested, juiced

50ml olive oil
HERB SAUCE
¼ cup dill, chopped
½ cup basil, chopped
¼ cup mint, chopped
½ lemon, zested, juiced
100ml olive oil

1 Heat 1 tbs of the olive oil in a large frying pan over medium heat. Add the prosciutto and breadcrumbs and cook, stirring, until golden and crisp. Remove from pan and set aside.

2 Mix together chilli, mint, basil, garlic and olive oil. Rub all over steaks and leave for 20 minutes.

3 To make tomato ravioli, heat the olive oil in a large frying pan over medium heat and cook the onion and garlic for 3 minutes or until just soft. Add cherry tomatoes and cook, turning often, for 3 minutes or until softened. Season with salt and pepper, then cool.

4 Lay a gow gee wrapper on work surface; place 1 tbs of tomato mixture in centre of wrapper. Moisten edge with a little water and fold over to enclose and make a semi-circle, pressing firmly to seal. Fill remaining wrappers. Place in one layer on a tray and cover with plastic wrap.

5 To make coriander pesto, process coriander, sesame seeds, lemon zest and juice in a food processor until finely chopped. Slowly add oil, with motor running, until well combined. Season.

6 To make herb sauce, blend all ingredients in a blender until combined. Season and set aside.

7 Heat remaining oil in a large frying pan over medium–high heat and cook steaks for 4 minutes each side for medium-rare or to your liking. Leave on a plate, loosely covered, for 10 minutes.

8 Cook ravioli in a large pan of boiling water for 3 minutes or until tender. Lift out with a slotted spoon to drain.

9 Place a spoonful of herb sauce on each plate and top with steak and two ravioli. Drizzle the ravioli with coriander pesto and scatter breadcrumbs and prosciutto over the plate.

TIP Dry-aged beef is available from selected butchers and online. If you can't find it, buy the best quality steak you can find.

Ellie's
SMOKED DUCK AND CHERRY CANAPES

Michael, who had the upper hand at the United Nations challenge, decided that Ellie would cook the smoked duck canapé by Marriott Marquis chef Armando Monterroso. Her dish claimed the most votes from diners, although Hayden was a close second – despite the fact that all the waiters hovered at smiling Ellie's bench, leaving him desperately calling for service.

2 smoked duck breast fillets*
1 Lebanese cucumber
1¹/₂ tbs mirin
10 cherries, pitted, finely diced

2 tbs chopped chives
Sliced spring onion and
   micro cress, to garnish

SAUCE
1¹/₂ tbs hoisin sauce
¹/₂ tsp finely grated ginger
¹/₂ tsp Sriracha hot sauce*

1 Remove skin from duck breast and finely dice flesh.
2 To make sauce, mix together all ingredients and season with salt.
3 Peel the cucumber, remove seeds and finely grate the flesh. Combine with mirin in a bowl and season with salt.
4 Mix together duck, cherries, chives and sauce.
5 To make canapés, divide duck mixture among serving spoons. Drain excess liquid from cucumber, then place a little on top of duck mixture. Garnish with spring onion and micro cress.

TIP **In the challenge,** Ellie had to cut up her duck and smoke the breast. You can buy smoked duck breast fillets at specialist poultry shops and selected butchers. **Sriracha hot sauce** is a Thai hot chilli sauce, available from Asian food shops.

This dish won Ellie her first-ever challenge. *'You're normally in the pressure test, aren't you?'* asked George, cheekily. *'Now it's Ellie versus the Big Apple,'* said Matt Preston.

Alana's
THAI BEEF SALAD CANAPES

Michael's reward for his delicious 43rd Street taco was to decide who would prepare which canapé in the UN challenge. He gave this Thai beef salad, by Marriott Marquis chef Armando Monterroso, to Alana. But his cunning plan to seize glory and nobble the opposition backfired somewhat, with Ellie, Hayden and Alana all plating up terrific trays of canapés.

1kg scotch fillet steak
1 coconut*
1/2 red capsicum, finely diced
15g micro coriander, plus extra
   sprigs, to serve
1 1/2 tbs extra virgin olive oil
30 baby cos lettuce leaves

TAMARIND VINAIGRETTE
90g tamarind concentrate*
1 1/2 tbs honey
2 tbs vegetable oil
THAI DRESSING
3 tsp Thai red curry paste
125ml (1/2 cup) coconut milk

2 limes, juiced
1/2 cup basil leaves
1/2 cup coriander leaves

1 **To make tamarind vinaigrette,** whisk together all the ingredients with 1 1/2 tbs water. Season with salt and pepper.
2 Trim the steak and cut into 3cm-thick pieces. Marinate in 60ml (1/4 cup) tamarind vinaigrette for 15 minutes.
3 Heat a chargrill pan over high heat and cook the beef for 3 minutes, turning once, for medium-rare. Set aside to rest for 15 minutes.
4 **To make Thai dressing,** process all ingredients in a food processor until well combined.
5 **To prepare coconut,** preheat the oven to 200°C. Pierce the eyes with a skewer and drain out the liquid. Bake the coconut for 20 minutes. Remove from the oven and leave until cool enough to handle. Reduce oven to 180°C.
6 Using a hammer, tap all around the centre of the coconut. Keep tapping until coconut splits open. Slide a non-serrated knife between the coconut flesh and the shell to remove chunks of flesh. Use a vegetable peeler to shave flakes from the flesh. Arrange on an oven tray and cook for 3 minutes or until lightly toasted. Thinly slice beef and toss with capsicum, micro coriander, olive oil and remaining tamarind vinaigrette.
7 **To make canapés,** arrange beef mixture onto small lettuce leaves and top with a drizzle of dressing, a shaving of coconut and a sprig of micro coriander.

TIP **Fresh coconut** gives a beautiful flavour, but you can use coconut flakes if necessary. For a special occasion, use Wagyu steak (as Alana did at the United Nations). **Tamarind concentrate** is available from supermarkets.

Serves **4-6**

Preparation **1 hour + 30 minutes resting**

Cooking **1 hour**

Chef Cesare Casella's
PASTA ALL'AMATRICIANA

Ellie had survived five elimination tests, but her win at the UN gave her the first chance for immunity. She was in a New York state of mind as she cooked against Cesare Casella in Central Park. 'You're going into a den with a Tuscan lion, who has the scent of rosemary all over him,' said guest judge Lidia Bastianich. Ellie emerged from the lion's den victorious.

ORECCHIETTE
400g (2½ cups) fine semolina, plus extra, to dust
1 tsp salt
½ tsp ground black pepper
2 eggs, lightly beaten
2 tbs extra virgin olive oil

2 tbs dry white wine
SAUCE
80ml (⅓ cup) extra virgin olive oil
2 red onions, thinly sliced
350g cured meat,* chopped
800g can diced tomatoes

80g (1 cup) grated pecorino romano
80g (1 cup) grated parmigiano reggiano
2 tbs chopped parsley

1 To make orecchiette, mix semolina, salt and pepper in a bowl and make a well in the centre. Add eggs, olive oil and wine and, using a fork, draw in flour from side until thick, then work in remaining flour with your hands. Add 1–2 tbs water if necessary. Turn out onto a lightly floured surface and knead for 5 minutes or until dry and firm. Wrap in plastic and leave for 30 minutes.

2 Divide dough into 6 pieces. Roll each piece into a rope about 1.5cm thick. Cut each rope into 5mm rounds. Press each round with your thumb to make slightly concave discs. Place on a large tray and lightly dust with semolina. Cover with plastic wrap and refrigerate until required.

3 To make sauce, heat oil in a saucepan over medium heat and cook onion, stirring frequently, for 5 minutes or until soft but not coloured. Stir in the meat and cook for 5 minutes.

4 Stir in tomatoes and bring to the boil. Cook for 5 minutes, stirring frequently, then reduce heat to low and simmer, uncovered, for 40 minutes, stirring occasionally.

5 Cook orecchiette in a large saucepan of boiling salted water for 30 seconds. Drain, keeping 250ml (1 cup) of the cooking water.

6 Add pasta to sauce and cook over medium heat for 3 minutes or until pasta is al dente. Remove from heat and add most of the cheese and parsley. Stir vigorously, adding a little pasta water if needed to loosen the sauce. Sprinkle with remaining cheese and parsley to serve.

TIP Cesare used a combination of good-quality cured meats, such as parmacotto, prosciutto grigliato, prosciutto di Parma, mortadella di Bologna, speck Alto Adige, soppressata and guanciale. A good Italian deli should have these meats, or similar varieties.

THE DALAI LAMA'S LUNCH

A special guest is coming for lunch — cooking for the Dalai Lama brings out the very best in the kitchen. Autumn is the saddest season for Billy. Dani competes with an Olympian MasterChef on her own turf to win a second pin. Hayden's in pain in the Qantas Lounge and the nation weeps when the last boys in the competition give each other a farewell hug.

FILMING DIARY

Sunday

EPISODE 67 Making lunch for the Dalai Lama is a memory that will last for ever.

Monday

EPISODE 68 The autumn dessert sends Billy and his 'free-thinking' brain home.

Tuesday

EPISODE 69 It's game on with Eamon. Can Dani win a second immunity pin?

Wednesday

EPISODE 70 A last team challenge: deliver first-class food to first-class passengers.

Thursday

EPISODE 71 In a tough elimination, Kate, Michael and Hayden have an open pantry.

Friday

EPISODE 72 Only five are left for masterclass. George goes vegetarian.

Week 12

A VERY SPECIAL LUNCH GUEST

Billy grew up in a Buddhist family, and never imagined he'd be cooking for the Dalai Lama. The brief is to create the 'best, most joyful' vegetarian dish for his lunch.

Chef and Buddhist Kylie Kwong arrives as a mentor. 'It's not every day you get to cook for the 14th incarnation of a world spiritual leader,' says Matt Preston.

His Holiness arrives in the kitchen to meet the contestants. 'Clarity, vision – it's all gone out of the window,' says Dani. Billy's making Buddha's delight: 'The Dalai Lama touched me,' he whispers.

Ellie's gnocchi are 'mush' and she wants to run away. 'You wait until you see his reaction, it's alright,' Kylie reassures her.

What does the Dalai Lama think of his lunch? 'I think all monks, when they get food, are very happy!' He won't choose any dish over another and it's left to the judges to declare Dani victorious.

Below: Nothing goes right for Hayden in the 'First Lounge' challenge and the kitchen is in mayhem when the blue team arrives. But the reds have had similar disasters: 'Bun after bun is burning,' says team captain Alana as Dani overheats.

A LITTLE BIT SAD...

It's the last ever team challenge and Kate's 'a little bit sad. I'm going to miss them – in some weird, sick way'. Michael, Hayden and Kate battle against Alana, Dani and Ellie in the kitchen of Qantas First Lounge.

Alana's team serve first, handing over to Hayden's blues, who are worried about the state of the kitchen after Dani and Ellie have been in there: 'Those two are the dirtiest chefs in the kitchen.'

Michael's club sandwich and Kate's pork belly impress Neil Perry, but Hayden's day goes from bad to worse. Ellie drowns in dockets and Dani burns every other bun she cooks, but the reds win on flavour.

Kate, Michael and Hayden's elimination dishes are 'insanely good', but one has to go. Young women around Australia sob in front of their screens... Hayden's leaving the kitchen to go and catch some waves.

Below: 'Your Holiness, today I had a bit of a disaster in the kitchen,' Ellie tells the Dalai Lama. The gnocchi she cooks so often for her family turn to 'mush' in the challenge to make lunch for a spiritual leader who can't judge but 'adores food'.

'Today's challenge is about the giving and offering of food, and enjoying it.' Alana

ELLIE'S CHICKEN & DANI'S PIN

Ellie's made it through five pressure tests so far, but decides to use her immunity pin against Kate and Billy. Gary flaps his arms and clucks like a chicken. But, when Ellie sees Katrina Kanetani's intricate 'autumn' dessert, her relief is evident and it's Billy who's heading home.

Dani cooks against 2010 celebrity MasterChef Eamon Sullivan. He brings in his cookbook version of the chocolate delice that won him three perfect 10s in the final, but then drops a blender blade into his food processor and nearly blows himself up. 'It's like diving off the blocks and losing his togs,' says Hayden. Dani matches Eamon's score of three 8s and wins herself a second immunity pin.

Dani's
SRI LANKAN VEGETABLE CURRIES

Coriander, warmed roti and
  steamed basmati rice, to serve
DHAL
400g (2 cups) yellow split peas
2 tsp ground turmeric
2 tbs coconut oil
1½ tsp mustard seeds
1 tsp dried chilli flakes
1 tsp cumin seeds
2 sprigs fresh curry leaves
3 cloves garlic, crushed
250ml (1 cup) coconut milk
POTATO CURRY
½ tsp yellow mustard seeds
1 tsp fennel seeds
1 tsp cumin seeds
¼ tsp fenugreek seeds

2 tbs coconut oil
1 white onion, finely chopped
1 tsp ground turmeric
1 tsp dried chilli flakes
400g baby chat potatoes,
  quartered
150ml coconut milk
2 tsp garam masala
GREEN BEAN CURRY
1 tsp coriander seeds
1 tsp cumin seeds
½ tsp fennel seeds
¼ tsp fenugreek seeds
1 clove
½ tsp ground cinnamon
½ tsp ground turmeric
½ tsp garam masala

2 tbs coconut oil
1 white onion, finely chopped
4 cloves garlic, crushed
2 sprigs fresh curry leaves
1 pandan leaf, tied in a knot
400ml coconut milk
500g green beans, trimmed
COCONUT SAMBAL
150g (1 cup) grated coconut
  (fresh or frozen)
1 cup coriander, finely chopped
1½ cups mint, finely chopped
½ lime, juiced
1 long green chilli, seeded,
  finely chopped

1 To make dhal, rinse peas thoroughly, then put in a large saucepan with turmeric and 1.5L water.
Bring to the boil, reduce heat to low–medium and skim surface. Simmer, uncovered, for
35 minutes or until peas are tender and water has almost all evaporated.

2 Heat coconut oil in a frying pan over medium heat and cook spices, curry leaves and garlic,
stirring occasionally, for 3 minutes or until fragrant. Add to saucepan. Stir in coconut milk and
cook for a further 5 minutes. Season with salt and a little sugar to taste.

3 To make potato curry, fry all seeds in a dry frying pan over medium heat for 1 minute or until
fragrant. Cool, then grind to a fine powder. Heat coconut oil in a frying pan over medium heat
and cook the onion for 5 minutes or until soft. Add spice powder, turmeric and chilli flakes and
cook for 2 minutes or until fragrant. Stir in potatoes and 250ml (1 cup) water.

4 Cover and bring to the boil, then reduce heat to low and simmer for 10 minutes or until
potatoes are tender. Uncover and cook for 5 minutes or until liquid has reduced. Stir in coconut
milk and garam masala and cook for 2 minutes. Season with salt.

5 To make green bean curry, fry all seeds and the clove in a dry frying pan over medium heat for
1 minute or until fragrant. Cool, then grind to a fine powder with a mortar and pestle. Transfer
to a bowl. Stir in remaining spices and a pinch of salt.

6 Heat coconut oil in a frying pan over medium heat and cook onion and garlic for 5 minutes
or until soft. Add ground spice mixture, curry and pandan leaves and cook for 2 minutes. Stir
in coconut milk and 125ml (½ cup) water, then add beans and bring to the boil. Cook for
8 minutes or until beans are just tender. Season with salt and a little sugar.

7 To make coconut sambal, combine all ingredients in a bowl and season with salt.

8 Scatter curries with chopped coriander and serve with roti and steamed rice.

'A beautifully balanced dish
– six elements, all perfectly
executed.' Matt Preston

Serves **8**
Preparation **1 hour**
Cooking **1½ hours**

Michael's
GOAT'S CHEESE TORTELLINI WITH BEETROOT

Chives, goat's cheese, extra virgin olive oil, to serve

BEETROOT PUREE
2 x 200g beetroot, trimmed
125ml (½ cup) thickened cream
½ lemon, zested

BEETROOT BROTH
1kg beetroot, peeled, cut into 2cm pieces
2 tbs olive oil
1.5L vegetable stock
1 tsp fennel seeds
1 tbs grated horseradish*

ROASTED BABY BEETROOT
15 baby beetroot, trimmed
2 tbs olive oil

PASTA DOUGH
250g (1⅔ cups) '00' flour
6 egg yolks
1 egg
1 tbs milk
2 tsp olive oil

FILLING
250g soft goat's cheese
2 tbs finely chopped chives
1 tbs finely grated lemon zest
60ml (¼ cup) thickened cream

CANDIED WALNUTS
1½ tbs caster sugar
30g walnut pieces

1 **To make beetroot purée,** cook beetroot in boiling water for 1 hour 15 minutes or until tender. Drain and cool slightly, then peel. Finely grate beetroot, place in a small saucepan with cream and simmer for 5 minutes, then purée until smooth. Stir in lemon zest and season.
2 **To make beetroot broth,** preheat oven to 200°C. Put beetroot in roasting pan, drizzle with oil and roast for 40 minutes or until tender. Transfer to a large saucepan, add stock and fennel seeds and bring to the boil. Reduce heat to low and simmer, uncovered, for 30 minutes. Cool, then purée until smooth. Strain, return to a clean saucepan, stir in horseradish and season.
3 **For roasted baby beetroot,** place beetroot on an oven tray and drizzle with oil. Roast for 40 minutes or until tender. Cool, then slip off skins and cut in half.
4 **To make pasta dough,** place flour and a pinch of salt in a bowl and make a well in the centre. Mix egg yolks, egg, milk and oil and add to flour. Using a fork, draw in flour until thick, then work in remaining flour using your hands. Turn out onto a lightly floured surface and knead for 6 minutes or until smooth. Wrap in plastic and leave to rest for 30 minutes.
5 **For filling,** mix together ingredients, season with salt and pepper and refrigerate until needed.
6 **To make tortellini,** divide dough into 4 pieces and wrap in plastic. Using a rolling pin, flatten one portion to 3mm thick and 12cm wide. Set pasta machine at widest setting, then feed dough through, narrowing settings one notch at a time until at second thinnest setting. Repeat with remaining dough portions. Using a 10cm round cutter, cut 32 rounds from the dough. Place 1½ tsp of filling in centre of each round. Moisten edges with water and fold over to make a semi-circle, pressing firmly to seal. Bring ends together and press firmly. Place on a tray and cover with plastic wrap.
7 **To make candied walnuts,** put sugar and 2 tsp water in a small saucepan. Stir over low heat without boiling until sugar dissolves. Bring to the boil and cook for 8 minutes or until golden. Stir in walnuts. Pour onto a lightly oiled oven tray and leave for 10 minutes to cool and set.
8 Cook tortellini in 2 batches in boiling salted water for 3 minutes or until it floats to the surface.
9 **To serve,** spread beetroot purée onto plate and top with tortellini and baby beetroot. Sprinkle with walnuts, chives and goat's cheese, drizzle with extra virgin olive oil and serve with broth.

TIP **Use fresh horseradish,** if you can find it. **Grated horseradish** is available in jars at delis and supermarkets.

Serves **8**

Preparation 1½ **hours** + 1½ **hours** setting

Cooking **30 minutes**

Eamon Sullivan's
CHOCOLATE DELICE

PANNA COTTA
250ml (1 cup) thickened cream
125ml (½ cup) milk
55g (¼ cup firmly packed) brown sugar
½ vanilla bean, split, seeds scraped
2 tsp powdered gelatine

CHOCOLATE MOUSSE
2 tsp powdered gelatine

500ml (2 cups) thickened cream
75g (⅓ cup) caster sugar
35g (⅓ cup) dark (Dutch) cocoa
60g dark chocolate (70% cocoa solids), finely chopped

SALTED CARAMEL SAUCE
110g (½ cup) caster sugar
80ml (⅓ cup) thickened cream
75g unsalted butter, cut into 1cm pieces

ALMOND TUILES
45g unsalted butter
40g liquid glucose
75g (⅓ cup) caster sugar
35g (1¼ cup) plain flour
25g (¼ cup) flaked almonds

CHOCOLATE GLAZE
125ml (½ cup) thickened cream
100g dark chocolate (70% cocoa solids), finely chopped

1 To make panna cotta, place cream, milk, sugar and vanilla bean and seeds in a small saucepan and bring almost to the boil; remove from heat. Stir gelatine with 1 tbs boiling water until dissolved, then add to pan and stir. Leave for 20 minutes for flavours to infuse. Strain, discarding bean. Pour into eight 180ml (¾-cup) glasses. Refrigerate for 1 hour or until set.

2 To make chocolate mousse, stir gelatine into 2 tbs boiling water until dissolved. Place 125ml (½ cup) cream and 125ml (½ cup) water in a saucepan. Sift sugar and cocoa over cream mixture, then whisk until smooth. Stir over medium heat until sugar dissolves and mixture comes to a simmer. Remove from heat, then stir in gelatine until dissolved. Cool for 1 minute, then stir in chocolate until smooth. Strain, then refrigerate for 1 hour or until set.

3 Whisk remaining 375ml (1½ cups) cream to soft peaks. Add one-quarter of whipped cream to chocolate mixture and whisk well. Fold in remaining whipped cream. Transfer mousse to a piping bag fitted with a plain nozzle. Refrigerate until needed.

4 To make salted caramel sauce, put sugar and 60ml (¼ cup) water in a saucepan and stir over medium heat until sugar dissolves. Using a wet pastry brush, brush down side of pan to prevent sugar crystals forming. Bring to the boil, then cook, swirling pan occasionally but not stirring, until a dark golden caramel. Remove from heat and immediately stir in cream (take care as it will spit). Cool for 2 minutes. Whisk in butter one piece at a time. Add a pinch of salt. Cool.

5 To make almond tuiles, preheat oven to 180°C. Line a large oven tray with baking paper. Place butter, glucose and sugar in a small saucepan. Stir over low–medium heat until sugar dissolves. Bring to the boil, then remove from heat. Stir in flour and almonds. Spoon eight ½ teaspoons of mixture, 10cm apart, onto tray. Bake for 5 minutes or until golden. Cool tuiles on tray, then gently lift off and store in an airtight container until needed.

6 To make chocolate glaze, place cream in a small pan and bring to the boil over medium heat. Remove from heat and stir in chocolate until smooth.

7 To serve, pour caramel sauce over panna cotta in glasses and refrigerate for 15 minutes or until set. Pipe mousse over caramel, then, using a teaspoon dipped in hot water, smooth surface. Pour glaze over mousse, then tap glasses on work surface to level. Refrigerate for 15 minutes to set and serve with tuiles.

'That's making my neck tingle!
That's gorgeous!' Gary

Serves **4**
Preparation **20 minutes**
Cooking **30 minutes**

Alana's
TEA-SMOKED SALMON
WITH ORANGE VINAIGRETTE

Alana and Hayden were captains in the final team challenge and went head-to-head in a mystery box test. Gary loved Alana's perfectly cooked salmon and 'knockout' combination of bitter leaves and citrus dressing. Hayden's downfall had begun...

TEA-SMOKED SALMON
20g (¼ cup) green tea leaves
1½ tbs caster sugar
Zest of ½ orange, cut into wide strips, pith removed
2 x 400g salmon fillets, skin on, pin-boned*

ORANGE VINAIGRETTE
1 orange, juiced
60ml (¼ cup) chardonnay vinegar
1 tbs extra virgin olive oil
SALAD
Vegetable oil, to shallow-fry

4 kipfler potatoes, thickly sliced
2 witlof, leaves separated
4 baby radishes, thinly sliced
Micro parsley, to serve

1 **To make tea-smoked salmon,** line a wok with 2 sheets of foil. Spread tea, sugar and orange zest over foil. Heat over high heat for 5 minutes or until mixture begins to smoke. Reduce heat to medium, place a lightly oiled rack in the wok and place salmon on the rack. Cover and smoke for 12 minutes.
2 Remove salmon from the wok and carefully peel off the skin. Set flesh aside, loosely covered with foil. Cut the skin into thin strips.
3 **To make orange vinaigrette,** mix juice and vinegar in a small saucepan. Bring to the boil, then reduce heat to low–medium and simmer for 4 minutes or until reduced by half. Whisk in olive oil and season with salt and pepper.
4 **For salad,** heat 5mm oil in a large frying pan and cook the potato slices for 6 minutes on each side or until tender and golden. Drain on paper towel. Add salmon skin to hot oil and cook for 5 minutes or until crisp. Drain on paper towel.
5 Flake salmon into large pieces. Arrange witlof, radish slices and potatoes on plates and top with salmon. Drizzle with vinaigrette and scatter with crispy salmon skin and parsley.

TIP **To pin-bone** the fish is to remove all the small bones (see cooking notes, page 264).

Michael's
SOUS-VIDE CHICKEN WITH PEA PUREE

4 chicken breast fillets
4 cloves garlic, chopped
1 bunch thyme
60g butter
2 tbs extra virgin olive oil
2 chicken thigh cutlets
80ml (⅓ cup) olive oil

2 carrots, chopped
4 celery stalks, chopped
1 large onion, chopped
250ml (1 cup) dry white wine
500ml (2 cups) beef stock
500g frozen peas
180ml (¾ cup) pouring cream

Zest of ½ lemon
1 bunch baby carrots, stalks
  trimmed, peeled
Micro herbs and sliced radish,
  to serve

1 Heat a large saucepan of water to 65°C, using a sugar thermometer to check the temperature. Season chicken with salt and pepper, then place each breast in a snap-lock sandwich bag. Add a pinch of garlic, 2 thyme sprigs, 10g butter and 2 tsp extra virgin olive oil to each bag. Expel all the air from bags and seal tightly. Place bags in saucepan, fully immersed in water. Cook, turning once, for 35 minutes or until cooked through* (monitoring heat to ensure water temperature doesn't fall below 62°C or go above 65°C). Remove bags from water.

2 Meanwhile, remove skin from chicken thighs, pat dry with paper towel and set aside. Roughly cut up thighs, exposing bones. Heat 2 tbs olive oil in a large deep frying pan over high heat and cook thighs for 10 minutes or until golden. Add carrot, celery and onion and season with salt. Cook, stirring continuously, for 10 minutes or until caramelised. Add remaining garlic and most of thyme to pan, then pour in wine. Cook for 5 minutes or until liquid has almost evaporated. Add stock and bring to the boil, then reduce heat to medium and simmer for 30 minutes or until reduced by three-quarters. Strain through a fine sieve lined with muslin and keep warm.

3 Meanwhile, preheat fan grill to very high. Flatten chicken skin to an even thickness. Place on a wire rack, season with salt and place another wire rack on top. Place under grill for 2 minutes or until golden and crisp. Set aside to cool, then break into pieces.

4 To make pea purée, cook 400g peas in boiling salted water for 2 minutes or until tender. Process peas, cream and lemon zest in a food processor until smooth. Season and press through a fine sieve. Keep warm.

5 Place remaining butter in a wide saucepan with 375ml (1½ cups) water, 1 sprig thyme and a pinch of salt. Cover and bring to the boil over medium heat. Add carrots and cook, covered, for 10 minutes or until just tender. Add remaining peas and cook for 2 minutes to heat through. Keep warm.

6 To serve, heat remaining oil in a large frying pan over medium heat and cook chicken breasts, skin-side-down, for 2 minutes or until skin is crisp and golden. Remove from pan and slice thickly. Spoon pea purée onto plates, top with chicken, crispy skin, baby carrots and whole peas. Drizzle with sauce and scatter with micro herbs and sliced radish.

TIP The chicken will have changed colour all the way through without any sign of pink, although it won't have as solid a texture as chicken cooked in an oven or frying pan.

Kate's
ALMOND-STUFFED SQUAB
WITH PARSNIP PUREE

4 x 500g squab, tunnel-boned,*
   trimmings reserved
2 tbs olive oil
30g butter
JUS
1 tbs olive oil
2 chicken wings, chopped
1 carrot, chopped
1 stalk celery, chopped
2 eschalots, chopped
1 leek, chopped
125ml (½ cup) dry white wine

1 tsp verjuice
STUFFING
1 pear, peeled, cored, chopped
1 tbs sangiovese verjuice
4 slices (140g) bread, torn
110g (²⁄₃ cup) blanched almonds
1 tbs finely chopped thyme
2 tbs finely chopped parsley
20g butter, finely diced
1 egg, lightly beaten
PARSNIP PUREE
3 parsnips, peeled, thickly sliced

250ml (1 cup) milk
2 sprigs thyme
20g butter
HERB SALAD
1 punnet micro cress
1 basil leaf, finely chopped
3 chives, finely chopped
1 tbs olive oil
1 tsp verjuice
1 tsp vincotto

1 **To make jus,** heat the olive oil in a frying pan over medium heat and cook squab trimmings and chicken wings for 8 minutes or until well browned. Add vegetables and cook for 8 minutes or until caramelised. Deglaze pan with wine and cook for 2 minutes. Add 500ml (2 cups) water and bring to the boil. Reduce heat to low and simmer for 30 minutes. Strain through a muslin-lined sieve into a saucepan and bring to the boil over medium heat. Reduce heat slightly and simmer for 10 minutes or until reduced by half. Season with salt and pepper and add verjuice.

2 **To make stuffing,** preheat oven to 200°C. Combine pear and verjuice and set aside. Process bread in food processor to coarse crumbs and transfer to a bowl. Process almonds and add to breadcrumbs with the herbs. Add pear and butter, then mix in enough egg to bind mixture without making it too wet. Season.

3 Pat squab dry inside and out with paper towel. Rub inside with a little of the olive oil and salt. Spoon stuffing into the cavity. Truss bird with string to keep its shape, then rub skin with a little more oil and salt. Heat remaining oil and butter in an ovenproof frying pan over medium heat and cook squab for 6 minutes, turning often, or until skin is golden brown. Transfer to the oven and cook for 15 minutes or until cooked through. Set aside for 10 minutes and remove string.

4 **To make parsnip purée,** combine parsnip, milk and thyme in a saucepan, cover the surface with a circle of baking paper and simmer for 15 minutes or until very tender. Drain, keeping cooking liquid. Process parsnip in a food processor until smooth, adding a little of the reserved liquid if needed. Return to a clean saucepan, add butter and heat gently. Season.

5 **To make herb salad,** trim micro cress from the punnet and toss with basil and chives. Whisk together olive oil, verjuice and vincotto and toss with salad. Season.

6 Place a spoonful of purée on each plate, top with the squab and drizzle with jus. Scatter herb salad over the squab and serve immediately.

TIP Ask your butcher to tunnel-bone the squab by removing the bones from the body of the bird (not the wings and legs) without tearing the skin or flesh. Substitute spatchcock (or poussin) for squab.

'The stuffing is delicious and that jus is supersweet and very complex. Clever cooking!' Gary

Hayden's
SESAME-CRUSTED CORAL TROUT

¼ daikon, peeled
1 tsp salt
1 tsp sugar
95g (½ cup) tapioca pearls
70g (1 cup) fresh breadcrumbs
1 tbs white sesame seeds
1 tbs black sesame seeds
Grape seed oil, to fry
4 x 175g coral trout fillets, skin on
2 yellow squash, quartered,
   steamed

3 baby radishes, finely sliced
BROTH
2 tbs grape seed oil
2 chicken wings, chopped
2 chicken drumsticks, chopped
2 eschalots, finely chopped
1 celery heart, chopped
250ml (1 cup) sake
150ml chicken stock
4cm piece ginger, thinly sliced
4 dried shiitake mushrooms

1½ tbs light soy sauce
1 tbs mirin
1 strip kombu (2 x 10cm)*
2 tsp cornflour
GARLIC WASABI CREAM
40g butter
5 cloves garlic, peeled
300ml milk
1 tsp agar agar*
¾ tsp wasabi powder*

1 Cut daikon into 4cm lengths and slice thinly lengthwise. Toss with salt and sugar and set aside.

2 To make broth, heat oil in a deep frying pan and cook chicken over medium heat for 10 minutes or until starting to brown. Add eschalot and celery and cook for 2 minutes or until lightly browned. Deglaze pan with sake and bring to a simmer for 4 minutes or until reduced by half.

3 Strain and return liquid to a saucepan with stock, ginger, mushrooms, soy sauce, mirin and 200ml water. Bring to the boil, reduce the heat to low–medium and simmer for 5 minutes or until slightly reduced. Turn off heat and add kombu. Leave for 20 minutes to infuse.

4 Strain through a muslin-lined sieve into a small frying pan. Mix cornflour with 1 tbs water until smooth; add to the pan and bring to the boil. Cook for 2 minutes or until thickened slightly.

5 To make garlic wasabi cream, melt butter in a saucepan over low heat, then cook garlic for 2 minutes or until soft but not coloured. Add milk, bring to a simmer, then reduce the heat to very low. Cook for 5 minutes to flavour milk. Strain into a clean pan over low–medium heat, add agar agar and whisk until dissolved and almost at boiling point. Strain into a bowl and refrigerate for 20 minutes or until softly set. Whisk cream to a smooth paste, then whisk in wasabi powder and season. Spoon into a piping bag and refrigerate until needed.

6 Bring a large saucepan of water to the boil. Add tapioca pearls and stir to remove any lumps. Cook for 10 minutes or until tender and with a speck of white starch in the centre of each pearl. Transfer to a sieve and rinse under cold running water. Set aside.

7 Preheat oven to 180°C. Process breadcrumbs, sesame seeds and a pinch of salt in a processor. Rub fish with oil, then press breadcrumb mixture onto skin. Heat 3mm oil in an ovenproof frying pan over medium–high heat and cook fish, crumb-down, for 3 minutes or until golden. Turn over and transfer to oven for 3 minutes to just cook through. Set aside for 2 minutes.

8 Rinse daikon and pat dry. Arrange tapioca on plates and top with fish. Arrange vegetables around fish and pipe 3 small mounds of garlic cream onto each plate. Serve with the broth.

TIP Kombu is a type of dried kelp, available from Asian shops; as is **wasabi powder**. **Agar agar** is a vegetarian alternative to gelatine and is available from health food shops.

COOK FOR SOMEONE YOU LOVE

A special mystery box leads to Machiavellian behaviour and Michael finally gets a chance for immunity. Everyone's favourite day sees beloved guests in the kitchen and Alana winning a dream prize. The pyjama-clad Top 5 cook nightmare ingredients and the Ellie-minator is eliminated.

FILMING DIARY

Sunday

EPISODE 73 The 'kris kringle' mystery box messes with everyone's heads.

Monday

EPISODE 74 Alana wins a night at home with dinner cooked by Gary and George.

Tuesday

EPISODE 75 Michael misses immunity by just one point against Teage Ezard.

Wednesday

EPISODE 76 Salsify, sea urchin, pigs' tails... nightmare ingredients are in the house.

Thursday

EPISODE 77 Dani plays her immunity pin, leaving Alana and Ellie to fight it out.

Friday

EPISODE 78 A masterclass on 'plating' and Gary cooks 'Christmas in July'.

Week 13

MYSTERY BOX MADNESS

'This mystery box is going to mess with your heads.' Pick the ingredients for another contestant with just one thing in mind: strategy. 'Ha, yes, strategy... I know how to cook that,' grins Ellie.

Ellie picks for Dani, and gives a naughty cackle, because Dani's confided that she's not happy cooking Italian. Ellie loads her basket with choice Italian ingredients.

Michael's never had the chance to cook for immunity – and Kate's secretly picking dessert goodies to foil his chances again. Alana chooses a rabbit for Ellie. 'Alana gave me the basket from hell,' says Ellie, who's just enjoyed doing the same thing to Dani. 'There's going to be a rabbit head under her pillow tonight.' Alana's too preoccupied with her flounder to care.

Michael's stunning panna cotta shows he's beaten his dessert demons. He finally wins the chance to cook for immunity.

Below: 'These two ladies are the reason I am who I am.' Micha[e]['s] sister Ruth and mum Genevieve are thrilled at the idea of the prize on offer. When Kate runs out of time, George helps Luke[,] Erin, Liam and Maya make ham and pineapple pizzas.

doesn't gag,' says MIchael – not something he's ever had to consider at tasting.

Alana's crêpe stack wins and she heads home with Rob, the 'three chubby amigos' following to cook them a spectacular dinner. Alana scores them an 11 out of 10.

COOK YOUR NIGHTMARE

Everyone's at home in pyjamas when three top chefs arrive with five shockingly bizarre ingredients. Michael grabs the sea urchin, Ellie the salsify, Alana the pigs' tails and Dani the licorice. Kate gives the rest serious 'pumpkin-envy'. Michael spends a lot of time ferrying ingredients to his downstairs den; Alana's little piggy bones cause strife; and Ellie's salsify is a true disaster. Dani plays her immunity pin, leaving Alana to step into her place and send Ellie home just before finals week.

Clockwise from below: Ruth helps little brother Michael cook his lamb roast. She'll have 'a taste' of the lambs' brains; 'Dani gets a bit stressed sometimes,' says her mum. 'No?' says George. 'And she's messy.' 'NO?' George shouts in disbelief; Ellie's making chicken pie for her mum, Ann.

'Hold on to your hats. Hold on to your hearts, and welcome the people you love.' Matt Preston

CRYING – BUT IN A GOOD WAY!

'Today's guests will make Nigella and Heston pale in your memories.' Dani can't imagine who's coming: 'Barack Obama?' The sobbing starts as the Top 5 spot their loved ones through the window. Alana's husband, Rob, has lost 10kg: 'Let's just say the culinary standards have dropped in our house.' Dani and her look-alike mum, Jenny, don't let go of each other all day.

Kate's daughter, Maya, joins the judges and is taught how to give a steely stare from the front. 'You're much better looking than Matt Moran,' says George.

Kate is cooking pork because husband Luke thinks 'the pig makes the culinary world go round' and Ellie's mum comes down to clean her bench. But Michael's beautiful lamb brains aren't rapturously received by his squeamish sister: 'Ruth, can you get the brain down? I hope she

Serves **4**
Preparation **2 hours + setting**
Cooking **45 minutes**

Michael's
PANNA COTTA & ROASTED RHUBARB
WITH HONEY & ORANGE SAUCE

PANNA COTTA
500ml (2 cups) pouring cream
55g (¼ cup) caster sugar
Zest of ½ orange
½ tsp vanilla extract
2 x 5g titanium-strength
  gelatine leaves

ROASTED RHUBARB
2 stalks rhubarb
1½ tbs caster sugar
1 lemon, zested, juiced
COCONUT TUILES
25g (⅓ cup) shredded coconut
75g (⅓ cup) caster sugar

SWEET & SALTY ALMONDS
20 blanched whole almonds
2 tbs caster sugar
ORANGE & HONEY SAUCE
1 orange, zested, juiced
1½ tbs honey
1½ tbs caster sugar

1 To make panna cotta, put cream, sugar and zest in a saucepan over low–medium heat. Bring almost to the boil, then turn off heat and leave for 5 minutes to infuse. Stir in vanilla. Soak gelatine in cold water for 3 minutes, then squeeze out excess water. Stir into cream until dissolved. Strain into a jug and cool to room temperature, stirring to release the heat. Pour cream mixture into four 125ml (½-cup) lightly oiled dariole moulds and refrigerate for 4 hours or until set.

2 For roasted rhubarb, preheat oven to 160°C. Trim rhubarb and cut into 7cm lengths. Place in a small ovenproof dish and sprinkle with sugar, lemon zest and juice. Cover with foil and cook for 10 minutes or until just tender.

3 To make coconut tuiles, preheat oven to 200°C. Cook coconut in a dry frying pan, stirring, over low–medium heat until lightly golden. Spread onto an oven tray lined with baking paper. Place sugar and 80ml (⅓ cup) water in a small saucepan. Stir over low heat without boiling until sugar has dissolved. Increase heat and boil without stirring for 4 minutes or until golden. Pour over coconut and leave to cool and set. When cool, break into smaller pieces and process in a food processor to a fine powder.

4 Lightly grease a large oven tray and line with baking paper (the oil will hold the paper in place). Sift coconut powder and spoon 3 tsp into a 10cm cookie cutter. Spread out evenly. Remove cutter and repeat to make 4 rounds. Bake for 2 minutes or until melted. Leave to cool on tray.

5 To make sweet and salty almonds, cook almonds in a dry frying pan over low–medium heat, stirring frequently, for 3 minutes or until golden. Transfer to a plate. Heat sugar and a pinch of salt in the pan. Add 1 tbs water and swirl pan to dissolve sugar. Cook for 5 minutes or until light golden. Return almonds to the pan and toss to coat. Spread out on an oven tray lined with baking paper to cool.

6 To make orange and honey sauce, put all ingredients in a small saucepan over low heat and stir until sugar has dissolved. Bring to a simmer and cook for 5 minutes or until reduced and thickened slightly (it will thicken further on standing).

7 Turn out panna cottas and serve with rhubarb, tuiles, almonds and a little sauce.

Serves **4**
Preparation **35 minutes**
Cooking **45 minutes**

Kate's

SPICED FLOUNDER & SCAMPI WITH CURRY SAUCE

2 x 400g flounder

1 eschalot, peeled, roughly chopped

1 egg white, beaten

75g (1/2 cup) plain flour

1 tsp cumin seeds, toasted, ground*

1 tsp coriander seeds, toasted, ground*

80ml (1/3 cup) olive oil

40g butter

6 scampi, halved lengthwise

Shredded kaffir lime leaves, Thai basil leaves and lime cheeks, to serve

COCONUT CURRY SAUCE

3 garlic cloves, peeled, roughly chopped

5cm piece galangal, peeled, roughly chopped

3 large eschalots, peeled, roughly chopped

1 red chilli

1 tbs vegetable oil

1 tsp cumin seeds, toasted, ground*

1 tsp coriander seeds, toasted, ground*

2 kaffir lime leaves, shredded

125ml (1/2 cup) coconut milk

1/2 lime, juiced, plus extra, to taste

Sugar and fish sauce, to taste

1 Fillet the flounder, reserving bones and head (or ask your fishmonger to do this). Skin the fillets, cover with plastic wrap and refrigerate until required. Rinse bones and head and roughly chop. Place in a saucepan with eschalot and 2L water. Bring to a simmer over low heat and cook, uncovered, for 20 minutes. Strain the stock.

2 To make coconut curry sauce, put garlic, galangal, eschalots, chilli and 1 tsp salt in a food processor and process to a coarse paste.

3 Heat oil in a frying pan over medium heat and cook paste for 6 minutes or until fragrant and golden. Add ground seeds and cook for 1 minute. Pour in 250ml (1 cup) stock and bring to the boil over medium heat. Add kaffir lime leaves and simmer for 3 minutes or until liquid has almost evaporated. Stir in coconut milk and juice and simmer for 2 minutes. Remove from heat and cool slightly.

4 Pour curry sauce into a blender, blend until smooth and strain into a saucepan. Adjust flavour with lime juice, sugar and fish sauce until flavours are balanced.

5 Dip flounder fillets in egg white. Mix flour with ground spices and a pinch of salt. Dust flounder in spiced flour and shake off any excess.

6 Heat oil and butter in a large frying pan over medium heat and cook flounder for 1 1/2 minutes each side or until crisp and golden. Drain on paper towel. Add scampi to pan and cook for 2 minutes, shell-side-down. Turn and cook for 30 seconds or until cooked through.

7 Serve flounder fillets with 3 scampi halves and curry sauce. Scatter with shredded lime and basil leaves and serve with lime cheeks.

TIP **For the best flavour,** grind your spices with a mortar and pestle or use a spice grinder.

LEMON & SUGAR CREPE STACKS

ICE-CREAM
250ml (1 cup) milk
1 vanilla bean, split,
   seeds scraped
5 egg yolks
220g (1 cup) caster sugar
250g crème fraîche
350g can sweet
   chestnut purée
2 tbs Armagnac or brandy

LEMON CURD
4 egg yolks
75g (⅓ cup) caster sugar
3 tsp lemon zest
80ml (⅓ cup) lemon juice
60g unsalted butter, chopped
RASPBERRY SAUCE
125g raspberries
1 tbs caster sugar
½ vanilla bean, split,
   seeds scraped

CREPES
250g (1⅔ cups) plain flour
1 tsp caster sugar
2 eggs
410ml (1⅔ cups) milk
1 tsp unsalted butter, melted, plus
   extra to grease
ITALIAN MERINGUE
220g (1 cup) caster sugar
4 egg whites
Edible flowers, to serve

1 To make ice-cream, heat milk, vanilla bean and seeds in a small saucepan over medium heat until almost at boiling point. Remove from heat and discard vanilla bean.

2 Whisk yolks and sugar until pale. Pour hot milk onto yolk mixture in a slow stream, whisking continuously. Whisk in crème fraîche. Cover with plastic wrap and refrigerate for 3 hours.

3 Churn in an ice-cream machine until frozen. Transfer to an airtight container and freeze for 4 hours or until almost firm. Combine chestnut purée and Armagnac and stir through ice-cream to make ripples. Transfer to an airtight container and freeze for 4 hours or until firm.

4 To make lemon curd, whisk yolks and sugar in a small saucepan until pale. Add lemon zest, juice and butter and place over very low heat. Whisking continuously, cook for 8 minutes or until thickened. Strain into a bowl and cool slightly, stirring frequently to release the heat. Cover the surface with plastic wrap and leave to cool.

5 To make raspberry sauce, crush raspberries and mix with remaining ingredients. Strain.

6 To make crêpes, sift flour, sugar and a pinch of salt into a bowl and make a well in the centre. Whisk eggs, milk and 125ml (½ cup) water together and slowly pour into well, whisking until smooth. Stir in melted butter, cover with plastic wrap and leave for 20 minutes.

7 Heat a non-stick frying pan with 21cm base and lightly grease with butter. Pour 60ml (¼ cup) batter into pan, swirling to cover base. Cook for 1 minute each side or until lightly browned. Transfer to a plate and repeat with remaining mixture to make 12 crêpes.

8 To make Italian meringue, place sugar and 250ml (1 cup) water in a saucepan over medium heat and stir, without boiling, until sugar has dissolved. Bring to the boil. Cook for 6 minutes or until syrupy. Whisk egg whites with a pinch of salt in a large bowl until firm peaks form. Gradually add syrup in a thin stream, beating continuously. Whisk for 8 minutes or until cooled, thick and glossy. Transfer to a piping bag fitted with a plain 1cm nozzle.

9 Make 2 piles of 6 crepes. Use a 7cm cutter to cut 4 stacks from each pile. Separate crêpe rounds, reserving 8. Spread half the rounds with lemon curd and half with raspberry sauce. Make 8 stacks, alternating lemon curd and raspberry crêpes; top with reserved rounds. Pipe meringue on top and scorch with a blowtorch. Serve with ice-cream, lemon curd and flowers.

Serves **6**
Preparation **40 minutes + chilling**
Cooking **1 hour 20 minutes**

Ellie's
CHICKEN, LEEK & MUSHROOM PIE

SUET PASTRY
300g (2 cups) plain flour
125g fresh suet, grated
1 egg, lightly beaten, to glaze
FILLING
1 tbs olive oil
3 eschalots, finely chopped
1 carrot, chopped
1/2 leek, sliced
3 cloves garlic, finely chopped
2 tsp thyme leaves
750g chicken thigh fillets,
  trimmed, cut into 2cm pieces

2 tbs plain flour, seasoned
125ml (1/2 cup) white wine
180ml (3/4 cup) chicken stock
200g field mushrooms, chopped
125ml (1/2 cup) pouring cream
MASHED POTATO
750g sebago potatoes, peeled,
  cut into 5cm chunks
30g butter
100ml pouring cream
PEA PUREE
240g (2 cups) peas (fresh or
  frozen)

3 tsp mint leaves
125ml (1/2 cup) pouring cream
CAVOLO NERO
1 bunch cavolo nero, roughly
  chopped
1 tbs olive oil
1 clove garlic, chopped
5 anchovy fillets, finely chopped

1 **To make suet pastry,** process flour, suet and a pinch of salt in a food processor until mixture resembles crumbs. Add 125ml (1/2 cup) cold water and process until mixture just comes together. Divide into 2 portions: one about one-third of dough; and one about two-thirds of the dough – and shape each into a disc. Wrap in plastic wrap and refrigerate for 45 minutes.

2 Preheat oven to 180°C. Roll out the large pastry disc between 2 sheets of baking paper to about 4mm thick. Line base and sides of a 21cm round springform pan with pastry. Roll out smaller disc between 2 sheets of baking paper to 2mm thick and large enough to cover pan. Cover all pastry with plastic wrap and refrigerate until required.

3 **To make filling,** heat oil in a frying pan over medium heat and cook eschalots, carrot, leek, garlic and thyme for 8 minutes or until softened and caramelised. Toss chicken in seasoned flour until well coated. Add chicken and cook, stirring occasionally, for 5 minutes or until golden. Deglaze pan with wine and cook for 1 minute or until reduced slightly. Add chicken stock and mushrooms. Cook for a further 10 minutes or until reduced and thickened. Stir in cream and simmer for a further 5 minutes; season with salt and pepper and cool slightly. Transfer to a large bowl and leave for 15 minutes, stirring occasionally to release the heat. Cover with plastic wrap and refrigerate for 1 hour or until cold.

4 Spoon filling into pastry shell. Cover with pastry lid and press edges together firmly to seal. Trim edges. Cut a slit in the centre to let steam escape and brush lid with beaten egg. Bake for 45 minutes, cover top with foil and bake for a further 10 minutes or until golden.

5 **To make mashed potato,** cook potatoes in a large saucepan of boiling salted water for 15 minutes or until tender. Drain well and return to the pan. Mash with butter and cream.

6 **To make pea purée,** cook peas in boiling water for 3 minutes or until tender. Drain and process in a food processor with mint and cream until smooth. Season and warm through.

7 **For cavolo nero,** blanch cavolo nero in boiling water and drain well. Heat oil in a frying pan and cook cavolo nero, garlic and anchovies, stirring, for 2 minutes. Season.

8 Slice pie and serve with mash, pea purée and cavolo nero.

Dani's
VANILLA SLICE WITH RHUBARB & GINGER PUREE & BERRY SALAD

ROUGH PUFF PASTRY
400g (2²/₃ cups) plain flour
300g unsalted butter, diced
CREME PATISSIERE
500ml (2 cups) milk
2 vanilla beans, split,
 seeds scraped
3 egg yolks

75g (¹/₃ cup) caster sugar
75g (¹/₂ cup) cornflour
RHUBARB & GINGER PUREE
1 bunch rhubarb, chopped
¹/₂ tsp ground cinnamon
2cm piece ginger, grated
55g (¹/₄ cup) caster sugar
1 lemon, zested, juiced

PASSIONFRUIT ICING
225g (1³/₄ cups) icing sugar
60ml (¹/₄ cup) passionfruit pulp
BERRY SALAD
125g raspberries
125g blueberries
Micro mint leaves, to serve

1 **To make pastry,** place flour and butter in a bowl with a good pinch of salt and 200ml iced water and mix with a fork until just combined. Turn out onto bench, gather dough together and shape into a rectangle. With short side closest to you, roll out dough between 2 sheets of baking paper to a 5mm-thick rectangle. Starting from a short side, fold over one-third of the pastry to the centre; then fold over the one-third on the other end to make 3 layers. Turn the pastry 90 degrees to the right, and roll out again to a long rectangle, keeping the edges straight and the corners square. Fold into 3 layers again. Turn, roll and fold again. Repeat rolling, folding and turning 8 times to create layers in the pastry. Chill pastry between rolling if it gets too warm or soft. Wrap in plastic wrap and refrigerate for 30 minutes.

2 Preheat oven to 220°C and line 2 large oven trays with baking paper. Divide pastry in half, roll each half to a rectangle 20 x 30cm and put on trays. Prick all over and bake for 12 minutes or until crisp and golden. Remove from tray, roll once with a rolling pin to flatten and leave to cool.

3 **To make crème pâtissière,** combine milk, vanilla beans and seeds in a saucepan over low–medium heat. Slowly bring to almost boiling point. Whisk yolks, sugar and cornflour until pale. Slowly pour over the hot milk, whisking to combine. Strain through a fine sieve into a clean saucepan. Cook over medium heat, stirring, for 5 minutes or until custard boils and thickens. Transfer to a bowl. Cover surface with plastic wrap and leave to cool.

4 Grease a 16 x 26cm slice pan and line with baking paper, overhanging the long sides. Trim pastry to fit pan and place one piece in base. Spread crème patissière over pastry and lay other pastry sheet on top, flat-side-up. Cover with plastic and refrigerate for 30 minutes or until set.

5 **To make rhubarb and ginger purée,** place all ingredients in a saucepan over medium heat and bring to the boil. Cook for 5 minutes or until rhubarb has softened. Allow to cool, then transfer to a food processor and process until smooth.

6 **To make passionfruit icing,** sift icing sugar into a bowl and mix in passionfruit pulp until smooth. Spread over pastry top and leave for 15 minutes or until set.

7 **To make berry salad,** mix together all ingredients.

8 Lift vanilla slice from pan and cut into 8 pieces. Serve with purée and berry salad.

'You've taken the humble tuckshop vanilla slice back to its beginnings as a beautiful multi-layered French dessert' Matt Preston

Kate's
CARAMELISED PUMPKIN CAKE

CINNAMON MOUSSE

60ml (1/4 cup) milk

60ml (1/4 cup) pouring cream

2 cinnamon quills, toasted

1 tsp ground cinnamon

5 eggs, separated

110g (1/2 cup) caster sugar

10g gold-strength gelatine leaves

200g crème fraîche, beaten

PUMPKIN CAKE

280g butternut pumpkin, peeled,
   seeded, cut into 3cm chunks

50g butter, melted

2 tbs brown sugar

125g unsalted butter

275g (1 1/4 cups) caster sugar

2 eggs

225g (1 1/2 cups) self-raising flour

50g (1/2 cup) walnut halves

1 tbs maple syrup

SPICED SYRUP

1 cinnamon quill

1 star anise

1/2 tsp cumin seeds

1 tbs maple syrup

MAPLE BACON

6 slices prosciutto, thinly sliced

60ml (1/4 cup) maple syrup

CANDIED WALNUTS

50g (1/2 cup) walnut halves

1 **To make cinnamon mousse,** put milk, cream, quills and ground cinnamon in a saucepan and bring almost to the boil. Remove from heat; leave for 15 minutes to infuse. Discard quills.

2 Place egg yolks and half the sugar in a heatproof bowl over a pan of simmering water (don't let the bowl touch the water). Whisk for 5 minutes or until mixture holds a figure-of-eight trail.

3 Soften gelatine in cold water for 3 minutes, then squeeze out excess water. Stir into infused milk until dissolved. Whisk into egg mixture, then fold in crème fraîche.

4 Whisk egg whites to soft peaks, gradually beat in remaining sugar and gently fold into egg mixture. Cover with plastic wrap and refrigerate for 1 hour or until set.

5 **Meanwhile, to make cake,** preheat oven to 180°C. Put pumpkin on paper-lined oven tray, drizzle with combined butter and brown sugar and toss to coat. Bake for 30 minutes or until tender and caramelised. Cool, then purée until smooth.

6 Grease a 16 x 26cm slice pan and line with baking paper, overhanging the long sides. Beat butter and 55g sugar with electric beaters until pale and fluffy. Add eggs, one at a time, beating after each addition. Fold in pumpkin purée. Fold in flour and walnuts until just incorporated. Spoon into pan; smooth surface. Bake for 30 minutes or until springy to touch.

7 Put remaining caster sugar and 250ml (1 cup) water in a saucepan over medium heat. Stir until sugar has dissolved. Bring to the boil and cook for 5 minutes until syrupy. Combine 80ml (1/3 cup) sugar syrup with maple syrup and spoon over hot cake when removed from the oven.

8 **To make spiced syrup,** dry-fry spices over medium heat for 2 minutes or until fragrant, then grind to a powder. Put in a saucepan with 80ml (1/3 cup) of the remaining sugar syrup and maple syrup and leave for 5 minutes to infuse. Strain.

9 **To make maple bacon,** preheat oven to 180°C. Brush prosciutto with maple syrup and bake for 5 minutes between 2 sheets of baking paper, weighted down with an oven tray to keep it flat.

10 **To make candied walnuts,** place saucepan of remaining sugar syrup over medium heat and cook for 2 minutes or until lightly golden. Remove from heat, add walnuts and toss to coat. Separate nuts on a sheet of baking paper and leave to cool and set.

11 Serve cake with maple bacon, mousse, candied walnuts and a jug of spiced syrup.

Alana's
HARISSA LAMB WITH
FENNEL & CARROT SALAD

The challenge was 'fix your biggest stuff-up' and, for the judges, it was personal. 'You had to cook those dishes, but we had to eat them!' Ellie knew immediately what would come back to haunt her: the Spanish invention test, when Gary described her stuffed capsicum as 'strangely unpleasant'. Alana had had very few disasters and re-made her lamb cutlets from week 8. This time she cooked her lamb perfectly, and the Ellie-minator finally went home.

HARISSA LAMB
2 tbs harissa paste*
2 tbs olive oil
2 tbs orange juice
12 large lamb cutlets
FENNEL & CARROT SALAD
60ml (1/4 cup) sangiovese
  verjuice*

60ml (1/4 cup) orange juice
1 tsp chopped coriander
60ml (1/4 cup) extra virgin
  olive oil
2 tbs orange blossom water*
2 small fennel bulbs, thinly sliced
4 baby carrots, thinly sliced
1 tbs pine nuts, roasted

**PRESERVED LEMON
  GOAT'S CURD**
80g goat's curd
1 tbs preserved lemon rind,
  finely chopped
CUMIN SALT
1/2 tsp cumin seeds, toasted
1 tbs salt

1 To make harissa lamb, combine harissa paste, olive oil and orange juice. Remove skin from cutlets, leaving a thin layer of fat intact. If you like, French the bone (see cooking notes, page 264) so it is very clean. Rub marinade over meat and set aside for 10 minutes.

2 Heat a chargrill pan over high heat. Cook lamb in batches, fat-side-down, for 4 minutes or until fat has rendered and meat is browned. Turn to cook each side for 2 minutes or until just cooked. Transfer to a plate to rest for 10 minutes.

3 To make fennel and carrot salad, combine verjuice, orange juice, coriander, oil and orange blossom water and season with salt and pepper. Place fennel, carrot and pine nuts in a bowl, add dressing and toss to coat.

4 To make preserved lemon goat's curd, combine curd and lemon in a bowl. Season.

5 To make cumin salt, grind cumin seeds and salt together with a mortar and pestle.

6 Serve lamb cutlets with fennel and carrot salad, spoonfuls of preserved lemon goat's curd and a sprinkling of cumin salt.

TIP **Harissa paste** is a spicy paste of red chillies originally from Tunisia. **Verjuice** is an unfermented juice made from slightly under-ripe grapes. It is used in the same way as good vinegar. Sangiovese verjuice is made from Sangiovese grapes and is slightly sweeter. **Orange blossom water** is distilled from orange blossoms and is used in Middle Eastern cooking to add a sweet fragrance to food.

A NEW MASTERCHEF

The 'cookbook challenge' sees Michael win a secret meeting in the pantry — will he make the most of his advantage? Dani has a bad day and a frozen pot of autobiographical ice-cream sends her home. Alana loses her nerve at Marque and has to confront the MasterChef 'worst-case scenario'. Kate and Michael fight the final battle — all hail the new MasterChef!

FILMING DIARY

Sunday

EPISODE 79 Curtis Stone is in the kitchen as mentor for the 'cookbook challenge'.

Monday

EPISODE 80 The 'smiling assassin' brings in her chook terrine for a pressure test.

Tuesday

EPISODE 81 Tell the story of your life with three special dishes. It's goodbye to Dani.

Wednesday

EPISODE 82 Keep your hat on... and cook a course in a three-hat Sydney restaurant.

Thursday

EPISODE 83 Alana's 'derelict' Adriano Zumbo house of horrors sends her home.

Friday

EPISODE 84 The last masterclass is playful – who's on the phone for Mat?

Sunday

EPISODE 85 Michael and Kate fight it out to become MasterChef 2011. A quick mystery box, the 'best dishes of their lives' and René Redzepi's 'snowman' dessert are their final tests. Who will earn the title?

Finals week

MICHAEL FEELING TRICKY

The 'cookbook challenge' has the Top 4 working overnight to write a recipe to satisfy Curtis Stone and the home cook. Dani's let down by her maths but Michael's chicken gives him a head start in the next day's pressure test. He cheekily leaves sugar and tart tins around to persuade the girls they're cooking an Adriano Zumbo dessert – and they fall for it. When kitchen favourite Maggie Beer enters, it's smiles all around... for a couple of minutes. 'Maggie's the ultimate smiling assassin,' says Alana, as she unveils her 'rather tricky chook terrine'. No-one cooks well and all four are in black aprons for an elimination test.

COOK YOUR LIFE STORY

Among the incredible autobiographical dishes lurks a disaster. Kate's ice-cream sandwich and Alana's chocolate indulgence are 'two of the best desserts

Below: It's a race to get to the first mystery box of the finale. There are three boxes and Kate and Michael must prepare ingredients from each in turn, before putting them together to make a spectacular dish. Michael takes an early lead.

THE GRAND FINALE

The heavy rain outside is fitting, because inside, a perfect MasterChef storm is brewing. Michael and Kate stand alone in the kitchen. Alone, apart from the dinner-suited judges, an array of Australia's finest chefs, and some 'mighty fine cooks', holding their breath on the balcony.

Michael's steak and oysters gives him an early lead in the mystery box race. 'You're cooking the dish of your life at the end of the ride of your life,' shouts Gary, and both Michael's lobster and Kate's quail live up to finale expectations.

This year's MasterChef clincher arrives in the shape of the 'snowman' dessert, carried by its creator, Noma's René Redzepi, the 'world's best chef'. Kate's near-perfect rendition of this super-tricky dessert wins her the 2011 MasterChef title.

Below: After a long week, Kate and Michael fight for the MasterChef title in front of their 22 competitors. Will René Redzepi's Noma 'snowman' defeat them? Of course it won't. Kate examines the crazy dessert carefully to ensure she gets every detail correct – George even eats the tiny carrot nose.

'Stop for one second to never forget this moment.' George

ever seen in this kitchen'. But Dani has to serve ice-cream frozen in the tin and it's time for the bubbly optimist to go home.

KEEP YOUR HAT ON

Alana is cooking a starter at Marque, Michael's in charge of a main course at est. and Kate is blissfully happy to make 'real' dessert for a gracious Peter Gilmore at Quay. Michael's beautiful roast venison is such a stunner that he goes straight into the Final 2, but Alana's nerves let her down for the first time and slicing smoked tuna becomes an insurmountable task.

Michael watches in safety from the balcony as 'torte torturer' Adriano Zumbo carries his extraordinary gingerbread house into the kitchen. It's knives, spray guns and boiled lollies at 20 paces, when Alana and Kate battle it out for a spot in the finale with Michael.

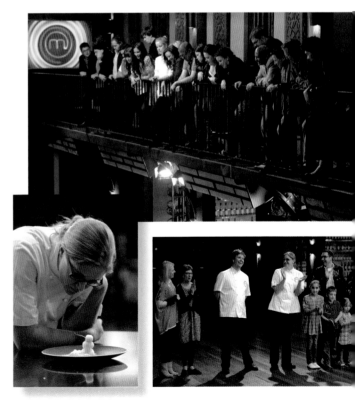

Michael's
NOT-JUST-ANOTHER SPRING CHICKEN

Michael's chicken, chargrilled cos and grape salad in the 'cookbook' challenge was such a big hit with his home tester, Sue, that she said she'd definitely buy any book he wrote! The flavours and simplicity of this lovely juicy salad won Michael the challenge, giving him a fantastic advantage in the Maggie Beer pressure test.

1.7kg chicken*
80ml (1/3 cup) olive oil
2 tsp thyme leaves
2 tsp lemon zest
4 baby cos lettuces
DRESSING
1 1/2 tbs lemon juice

60ml (1/4 cup) olive oil
1 tsp Dijon mustard
GRAPE SALAD
300g seedless red grapes,
    quartered lengthwise
1/2 small red onion, very
    thinly sliced

1/4 cup chopped flat-leaf parsley
1/4 cup chopped chives
110g (2/3 cup) blanched almonds,
    roasted,* chopped

1 Preheat oven to 220°C. Cut the chicken into 2 marylands (thigh plus drumstick) and 2 breasts on the bone. Drizzle 1 tbs of the oil in a large roasting pan and arrange chicken pieces, skin-side-up, in a single layer in the pan. Drizzle with 2 tbs oil and sprinkle with thyme and lemon zest. Season with salt. Roast for 25 minutes or until breasts are cooked through. Remove breasts from pan and cover loosely with foil. Roast marylands for a further 10 minutes or until cooked through. Set aside to rest, reserving pan juices.

2 Meanwhile, preheat a chargrill pan over high heat. Discard outer leaves of each lettuce and cut lettuce hearts lengthwise into quarters. Brush with remaining olive oil and season. Chargrill lettuce for 2 minutes on each side or until charred.

3 To make dressing, whisk together all ingredients and season.

4 To make grape salad, gently toss together all ingredients. Add dressing and toss again.

5 Cut marylands into thighs and drumsticks. Toss together chicken and lettuce, then arrange on a platter. Drizzle with pan juices, top with grape salad and serve immediately.

TIP **Ask your butcher** or poultry supplier to cut the chicken into portions if you're not confident doing it yourself. **To roast nuts,** spread on an oven tray and bake at 180°C for 5 minutes.

Serves **6**
Preparation **45 minutes** + chilling
Cooking **45 minutes**

Alana's
APPLE & ROSEMARY UPSIDE-DOWN TART

ROUGH PUFF PASTRY
150g (1 cup) plain flour
150g cold unsalted butter,
 roughly chopped
60ml (¼ cup) iced water
VANILLA CREME FRAICHE
200g crème fraîche

1 tbs icing sugar
1 vanilla bean, split,
 seeds scraped
CARAMEL APPLES
110g (½ cup) caster sugar
60ml (¼ cup) pouring cream
100g unsalted butter, chopped

3 x 5cm sprigs rosemary, plus
 extra, to garnish
1 vanilla bean, split, seeds
 scraped
4–5 small pink lady apples

1 To make pastry, put flour, butter and a good pinch of salt in a food processor. Mix in short
 bursts until mixture resembles coarse crumbs. Add iced water a little at a time, pulsing until
 mixture just comes together into a soft dough.

2 Turn out onto bench, gather dough together and shape into a rectangle. With short side
 closest to you, roll out dough between 2 sheets of baking paper to a 5mm-thick rectangle.
 Starting from a short side, fold over one-third of the pastry to the centre; then fold over
 one-third of the other end to make 3 layers. Turn the pastry 90 degrees to the right, and roll
 out again to a long rectangle, keeping the edges straight and the corners square. Fold into
 3 layers again. Turn, roll and fold again. Repeat rolling, folding and turning 8 times to create
 layers in the pastry. Chill pastry between rolling if it gets too warm or soft. Wrap in plastic wrap
 and refrigerate for 30 minutes. Preheat oven to 200°C.

3 To make vanilla crème fraîche, whisk together crème fraîche, sugar and vanilla seeds and
 refrigerate until required.

4 To make caramel apples, heat a large 21cm ovenproof non-stick frying pan over medium heat.
 Sprinkle sugar over base of pan, add 60ml (¼ cup) water and stir, without boiling, until sugar
 has dissolved. Bring to the boil, reduce the heat slightly and simmer, without stirring, for
 7 minutes or until dark golden. Remove from heat and stir in cream (take care as it will spit).
 Stir in butter, rosemary and vanilla seeds.

5 Cut apples crosswise into 1.5cm-thick slices and remove seeds. Lay apple slices in a single layer
 in the caramel, covering base of pan.

6 Roll out pastry to a 23cm round to snugly fit the frying pan. Lay pastry over apples, tucking
 down sides. Place pan over medium heat and bring to a simmer (don't worry if caramel begins
 to seep around pastry edge).

7 Place frying pan in the oven and cook for 35 minutes or until pastry is puffed and golden.

8 Remove from the oven and leave to stand for 1 minute. Place a large plate over the pan, and
 carefully invert so tart is apple-side-up on the plate. Tidy up any apples which may have
 moved, garnish with extra rosemary and serve with vanilla crème fraîche.

Kate's
WHITE CHOCOLATE ICE-CREAM SANDWICH

CARAMELISED WHITE CHOCOLATE
350g white chocolate, chopped
30g (¼ cup) skim milk powder
1 vanilla bean, split, seeds scraped

ICE-CREAM
350ml milk
100ml thickened cream
1 tsp vanilla bean paste

4 egg yolks
55g (¼ cup) caster sugar

HONEY WAFERS
25g unsalted butter, softened
2 tbs icing sugar
2½ tbs honey
50g (⅓ cup) plain flour

VINCOTTO PEARS
55g (¼ cup) caster sugar
1 tbs vincotto

2 pears, peeled

ORANGE CRUMBLE
25g unsalted butter
1½ tbs caster sugar
50g (⅓ cup) plain flour
Zest of ½ orange

WHITE CHOCOLATE CRUMBS
250g unsalted butter
50g (½ cup) skim milk powder

1 To make caramelised white chocolate, preheat oven to 180°C. Spread white chocolate, milk powder and vanilla seeds on a baking paper-lined oven tray. Place in oven for 3 minutes or until chocolate begins to melt. Remove from oven and stir with a silicon spatula, then return to oven for a further 3 minutes. Stir again. Repeat process 3 more times, or until mixture is darkly caramelised. Transfer to a plate and set aside.

2 To make ice-cream, put milk, cream and vanilla in a saucepan and heat until just below boiling point. Whisk egg yolks and sugar together until pale. Add 250g caramelised white chocolate to hot milk and stir until smooth. Set aside remaining white chocolate mixture to set hard. Pour hot cream mixture into yolks in a slow stream, whisking continuously. Strain into a clean saucepan and stir over low heat, without boiling, for 3 minutes or until mixture coats the back of a wooden spoon. Transfer to a bowl and leave for 10 minutes, stirring occasionally to release the heat. Cover with plastic wrap and refrigerate for 3 hours or until well chilled.

3 Churn in an ice-cream machine until frozen. Transfer to a 10 x 24cm foil-lined loaf pan, smooth surface, cover with plastic wrap and freeze for 3 hours or until firm.

4 To make honey wafers, preheat oven to 180°C. Mix all ingredients to a smooth paste. Spread thinly into a 24 x 28cm rectangle on a paper-lined oven tray. Bake for 6 minutes and then cut immediately into twelve 3 x 10cm rectangles.

5 To make vincotto pears, stir sugar, 50ml water and vincotto in a small saucepan over low heat, without boiling, until sugar dissolves. Increase heat and cook for 4 minutes or until reduced by half. Using a small melon baller, scoop balls from pears. Add to syrup, cover and cook for 1 minute. Turn off heat, leaving pears in syrup to continue cooking.

6 To make orange crumble, preheat oven to 100°C. Rub butter, sugar, flour and orange zest together. Wrap dough in plastic and freeze for 30 minutes or until firm. Finely grate onto a paper-lined oven tray and bake for 10 minutes or until dried out. Cool, then crumble.

7 To make white chocolate crumbs, cook butter and skim milk powder over low heat for 5 minutes or until light golden. Strain and spread solids on paper towel. Process remaining caramelised white chocolate to coarse crumbs; mix with butter solids and orange crumble.

8 Slice ice-cream into 8 bars. Place 1 honey wafer on plate, top with 1 ice-cream bar, 1 honey wafer, 1 ice-cream bar, then a final wafer. Serve with chocolate crumbs, pears and syrup.

'That is shiver-down-the-back-of-the-spine good!' Matt Preston

Alana's
CHOCOLATE INDULGENCE

Cocoa nibs,* raspberries, edible
  gold leaf* and edible flowers,
  to serve
MOUSSE
350g dark chocolate (70%
  cocoa solids)
165g (¾ cup) caster sugar
2 eggs

6 egg yolks
600ml cream, whipped
CHOCOLATE MUD CAKE
165g (¾ cup) caster sugar
300g dark chocolate (70%
  cocoa solids), chopped
150g unsalted butter, chopped
4 eggs, lightly beaten

300g (2 cups) plain flour
¾ tsp baking powder
HONEYCOMB
165g (¾ cup) caster sugar
70g liquid glucose*
2 tsp bicarbonate of soda

1 To make mousse, fill a saucepan one-third full with water and bring to a gentle simmer. Place chocolate in a heatproof bowl, place over pan and stir until melted (don't let the bowl touch the water). Stir until smooth, remove bowl from pan and cool slightly.

2 Combine sugar and 100ml water in a small saucepan over low heat and stir without boiling until sugar has dissolved. Bring to the boil and cook for 5 minutes or until slightly syrupy.

3 Using an electric mixer, beat eggs and egg yolks until pale and fluffy. With the motor running, slowly pour in the hot syrup, beating for 2 minutes or until cooled. Fold through the chocolate and whipped cream. Refrigerate for 1½ hours or until set.

4 To make chocolate mud cake, preheat oven to 150°C. Grease a 20cm square cake pan and line with baking paper. Fill a saucepan one-third full with water and bring to a simmer. Put sugar, chocolate, butter and 150ml water in a heatproof bowl, place over pan and stir until melted (don't let the bowl touch water). Stir until smooth, remove bowl from pan and cool slightly.

5 Whisk the eggs into the chocolate mixture. Sift flour and baking powder over the top and gently fold through. Pour into pan and bake for 20 minutes or until cake springs back to a gentle touch. Cool in pan for 5 minutes, then turn out onto a wire rack to cool completely.

6 To make honeycomb, grease a large oven tray and line with baking paper, so that paper overhangs the long sides. Combine sugar, glucose and 100ml water in a large saucepan. Stir over medium heat without boiling until the sugar has dissolved. Bring to the boil, then reduce heat to low-medium and simmer for 8 minutes or until mixture just turns light golden. Remove from heat.

7 Add bicarbonate of soda and quickly whisk into the sugar syrup – it will froth and bubble. Pour immediately into prepared tray (take care as it will become very hot). Set aside for 15 minutes or until cool and hard. Break up half the honeycomb and place in a food processor. Process to a fine powder. Break the remainder into shards.

8 To serve, cut cake into 12 pieces and place on plates. Serve with 2 quenelles of mousse and top with a shard of honeycomb. Sprinkle with honeycomb dust and decorate with cocoa nibs, raspberries, gold leaf and flowers.

TIP **Cocoa nibs** are roasted cocoa kernels found in specialist food shops. **Edible gold leaf** is from specialist food shops and cake decorating suppliers. **Liquid glucose** is from health food shops and selected supermarkets.

Michael's
'EST.' ROAST VENISON WITH BEETROOT

12 baby beetroot	CHESTNUT PUREE	100ml white wine vinegar
4 x 140g pieces venison saddle	50g butter	55g (¼ cup) sugar
1 tbs vegetable oil	250g peeled chestnuts* chopped	RED WINE JUNIPER SAUCE
Finely sliced blanched baby	180ml (¾ cup) pouring cream	200ml red wine
radishes and cress, to serve	PEARS	1 eschalot, chopped
SPICE CRUST	25g butter	2 thyme sprigs
1 tbs coriander seeds	1 large beurre bosc pear, peeled,	1 bay leaf
2 tsp black peppercorns	cut into eighths, cored	15 juniper berries
2 tsp juniper berries	1 tbs icing sugar	10 black peppercorns
½ tsp freshly ground nutmeg	PICKLED BEETROOT	100ml veal demi glace*
1 clove	1 medium beetroot	

1 **To make spice crust,** dry-fry coriander seeds over medium heat for 2 minutes or until fragrant. Mix with remaining ingredients and a good pinch of salt. Grind with a mortar and pestle.

2 **To make chestnut purée,** melt butter with 125ml (½ cup) water in a saucepan. Add chestnuts and cook over low heat, covered, for 25 minutes or until soft. Place in a food processor with half the cream. Process until combined, then add remaining cream in a slow stream, processing until smooth. Press through a fine sieve and set aside. Season with salt.

3 **For the pears,** melt butter in a frying pan over medium–high heat and add pear. Dust with icing sugar and cook, turning occasionally, for 3 minutes or until caramelised. Set aside.

4 **To make pickled beetroot,** cut top and bottom from the beetroot and slice very finely with a mandolin. Use a 5cm round cutter to cut neat discs from each slice. Place discs in a heatproof bowl. Heat vinegar and sugar in a small saucepan over medium heat. Stir, without boiling, until sugar has dissolved. Bring to the boil, then pour over beetroot discs and set aside to cool.

5 Preheat oven to 200°C. Place baby beetroot on a wire rack over a roasting pan. Pour 60ml (¼ cup) water into pan and cover with foil. Roast for 30 minutes until tender. Cool slightly; peel.

6 **To make red wine juniper sauce,** put wine, eschalot, herbs, juniper berries and peppercorns in a small saucepan over medium–high heat. Cook for 12 minutes or until reduced by three-quarters. Add demi glace and bring to a simmer. Season, then strain through a fine sieve and keep warm.

7 Preheat oven to 225°C. Coat venison generously with spice crust. Heat oil in a frying pan over high heat and sear the venison all over for 20 seconds each side. Transfer to a wire rack over an oven tray and roast for 4 minutes. Turn and cook for 4 minutes. Set aside to rest for 10 minutes.

8 **To serve,** warm chestnut purée and spread onto plates. Slice venison and place on top of purée. Add roasted baby beetroot, then decorate with pickled beetroot, radishes and cress. Serve with pears and red wine juniper sauce.

TIP **You can use** frozen chestnuts, or chestnuts from a jar, available from specialist food shops. Use fresh chestnuts when in season. **Demi glace** is a stock reduction, available from specialist food shops.

Serves **6**
Preparation **2 hours + 5 hours freezing**
Cooking **1 hour 15 minutes**

Kate's
'QUAY' COFFEE & CARDAMOM

ICE-CREAM
½ tsp cardamom seeds, crushed
180ml (¾ cup) milk
6 egg yolks
165g (¾ cup) caster sugar
125ml (½ cup) strong espresso
125ml (½ cup) pouring cream
KAHLUA MOUSSE
250ml (1 cup) milk
2 tbs Kahlua
2 x 5g titanium gelatine leaves

2 egg whites
110g (½ cup) caster sugar
250ml (1 cup) cream, whipped
VINCOTTO FIGS
55g (¼ cup) caster sugar
60ml (¼ cup) vincotto
100g semi-dried wild figs
COFFEE CRUMBS
50g (⅓ cup) plain flour
1½ tbs icing sugar
½ tsp ground coffee

30g cold unsalted butter,
   chopped
55g (⅓ cup) blanched almonds,
   roasted, finely chopped
60ml (¼ cup) strong espresso
1 tbs caster sugar
CARAMELISED ALMONDS
55g (¼ cup) caster sugar
25g butter
80g (½ cup) blanched almonds,
   toasted

1 To make ice-cream, heat cardamom seeds and milk in a saucepan until almost boiling. Turn off heat and leave to infuse for 5 minutes. Place egg yolks and sugar in a heatproof bowl over a pan of barely simmering water (don't let the bowl touch the water). Whisk for 5 minutes or until mixture holds a figure-of-eight. Strain milk and add to bowl with coffee and cream. Whisk for 5 minutes or until thickened enough to coat the back of a wooden spoon.

2 Remove bowl from pan and refrigerate for 10 minutes, stirring occasionally to release heat. Cover with plastic wrap and refrigerate for 2 hours. Churn in an ice-cream machine until frozen. Transfer to an airtight container and freeze for 3 hours or until firm.

3 To make mousse, put milk and Kahlua in a saucepan over medium heat. Bring almost to the boil; turn off heat. Soften gelatine in cold water for 3 minutes, then squeeze out excess water. Add to pan and whisk until dissolved. Transfer to a bowl and refrigerate for 10 minutes.

4 Whisk egg whites until soft peaks form. Beat in sugar a little at a time until thick and glossy. Fold together milk mixture, meringue and cream. Cover and refrigerate for 4 hours or until set.

5 For figs, put sugar, vincotto and 250ml (1 cup) water in a small saucepan over low heat. Stir until sugar has dissolved. Bring to a simmer, add figs and simmer gently for 20 minutes or until tender. Cool, then remove stems from figs and cut in half. Return to syrup until needed.

6 For coffee crumbs, preheat oven to 200°C. Process flour, icing sugar, coffee, butter and a pinch of salt into crumbs. Add 1½ tbs iced water and process until just comes together. Shape into a disc and roll out between 2 sheets of baking paper to 3mm thick. Freeze for 5 minutes. Place on a lined oven tray and bake for 12 minutes or until golden. Cool. Process to crumbs in food processor and mix with almonds. Stir coffee and sugar in pan over low heat until sugar dissolves. Bring to the boil; simmer for 2 minutes or until syrupy. Cool, then mix with crumbs.

7 For caramelised almonds, oil a wire rack and place over an oven tray. Stir sugar and 1½ tbs water in a small saucepan over low heat, without boiling, until sugar dissolves. Bring to the boil and cook, without stirring, for 5 minutes or until golden. Add butter and swirl pan until melted. Add almonds to caramel and swirl pan to coat. Tip onto oiled rack. Separate almonds and place on a paper-lined oven tray. Leave for 15 minutes or until set.

8 Scatter coffee crumbs on plate and top with mousse, ice-cream, figs and caramelised almonds.

Adriano Zumbo's
FAIRYTALE GINGERBREAD HOUSE

Adriano Zumbo had promised to return and the final elimination challenge was the perfect time for the MasterChef 'worst case scenario' to make an entrance. 'What is he carrying?' groaned Alana. 'I don't know whether to laugh, cry or crawl into the foetal position.'

Michael watched from the safety of the balcony, while Alana and Kate had 4½ hours to make this fully edible fairytale gingerbread house, complete with chocolate roof tiles, fruit jellies and crunchy praline 'brickwork'.

Kate had to remake her gingerbread after she burnt the first batch, while Alana thoroughly enjoyed making her own lollies. At the end it was relieved hugs all around. 'I think you'll be staying,' said Kate, but Alana disagreed: 'I've got squatters in my house and they've kicked in all the windows!'

It came down to taste, as always, and Kate's gingerbread won the day. But Alana had her own fairytale ending – she arrived home to find a houseful of friends dressed as Matt Preston.

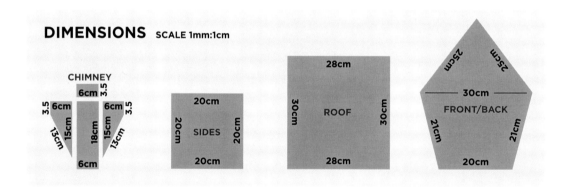

DIMENSIONS SCALE 1mm:1cm

CHIMNEY

6cm — 3.5
3.5 — 6cm — 6cm — 3.5
13cm — 15cm — 18cm — 15cm — 13cm
6cm

SIDES
20cm
20cm — 20cm
20cm

ROOF
28cm
30cm — 30cm
28cm

FRONT/BACK
25cm — 25cm
30cm
21cm — 21cm
20cm

'The one saving grace is that Alana looks just as horrified as I am!' Kate

Adriano Zumbo's
FAIRYTALE GINGERBREAD HOUSE

175g clear lemon
  boiled lollies
Caster sugar, to sprinkle
Cocoa, to dust
3 x 375g packets dark
  chocolate melts
350g hundreds and thousands
Assorted lollies and licorice
  ropes,* to decorate

GINGERBREAD
425g unsalted butter, chopped
440g (2 cups) caster sugar
500g glucose syrup
180ml (³/₄ cup) milk
1.2kg (8 cups) bread flour
2 tsp bicarbonate of soda
20g ground cinnamon
5 tsp ground cloves
5 tsp ground ginger

BRICKWORK
125g (1 cup) slivered almonds,
  roasted
200g (5 cups) corn flakes
500g Lindt Excellence Crunchy
  Caramel Milk Chocolate,
  chopped
125g unsalted butter, chopped

1 To make gingerbread, stir butter, sugar and glucose in a large saucepan over low–medium heat for 10 minutes or until sugar has dissolved. Stir in milk and remove from heat.

• Sift flour with bicarbonate of soda and spices into a large bowl, then add to milk mixture. Return pan to low heat, then stir (it will be stiff) until a paste-like consistency. Divide dough into four 450g and two 375g pieces. Flatten each piece into a square, wrap in plastic and refrigerate for 1 hour or until just firm.

2 To prepare glass for windows, process boiled lollies in a food processor to a fine powder.

3 To make stencils, scale up diagrams on previous page by 10 and use as guides to make 4 stencils (1 front/back, 1 roof, 1 side and 1 chimney) on cardboard or paper.

4 To make walls and roof, preheat oven to 180°C. Keep all trimmings for re-rolling. For back wall, roll out one 450g dough piece on a sheet of floured baking paper until 3mm thick. Using front/back stencil, cut out back wall. Transfer with paper to a large oven tray. Cut out a 6cm square window two-thirds up wall from base. Fill window hole with powdered lollies in a layer the same thickness as dough. Bake for 20 minutes for larger gingerbread pieces (15 minutes for smaller pieces) or until golden. Working quickly, scatter window with sugar for a frosted effect. Cool for 10 minutes on tray, then slide off with paper and cool completely.

• **To make front wall,** repeat rolling and cutting with another 450g dough piece and front/back stencil. Transfer with baking paper to tray. Carefully cut out a 5 x 10cm door at base of wall, making an arch at the top, and keeping the door. Cut out small windows from door. Using a small piece of trimmings, make a door knob. Transfer door to tray. Above door, cut out a 6cm square window. On both sides of door, cut out one window, 7cm high with a top width of 5cm and bottom of 2cm. Fill window holes with powdered lollies, bake, then frost glass, as before.

• **To make roof pieces,** roll out remaining two 450g dough pieces as before. Using roof stencil, cut out two roof pieces, then bake as before.

• **To make side walls,** roll out a 375g dough piece as before. Using side stencil, cut out one side wall, reserving trimmings. Transfer to tray with paper, then cut out a window 10cm wide x 4cm tall (it will become 2 windows once shutters are added). Fill window with powdered lollies, bake, then frost glass, as before. Repeat with remaining 375g dough piece.

5 To make chimney, shutters and eaves, roll out half the reserved trimmings as before. Using chimney stencil, cut out chimney pieces, then cut out a 5cm square for the door eave and two small right-angled triangles for eave supports. Roll out remaining trimmings, dust with cocoa, then roll cocoa into dough to colour. Cut out 12 shutter pieces, 2cm wide x 7cm high, and 4 shutter pieces, 2cm wide x 9cm high. Transfer to oven tray. Using a knife, mark shutters to create slats. Bake for 15 minutes or until golden.

6 **To make brickwork,** process almonds and corn flakes in a food processor to fine crumbs. Fill a large saucepan one-third full with water, bring to the boil, then reduce heat to low. Place chocolate, butter and 1 tsp sea salt flakes in a heatproof bowl, then place over pan (don't let the bowl touch the water). Stir until chocolate melts (don't let chocolate get too hot). Remove bowl from pan. Stir in almond mixture. Using an offset spatula or dinner knife, spread mixture thinly over front, back and side walls, avoiding windows. Using side of spatula, mark a brick pattern in mixture. Cool until set.

7 **To make chocolate roof tiles,** using a black marker, mark 3cm squares on a sheet of A4 paper to cover. Cover marked paper with a sheet of baking paper. Melt 1 packet of chocolate melts in a large heatproof bowl as before. Thinly spread chocolate over paper, leaving a 3cm border so you can see ends of marked lines. Shake paper gently to level, then scatter generously with hundreds and thousands. Cool until almost set. Following marked lines, cut the chocolate into tiles. Repeat layering and cutting with remaining melted chocolate and hundreds and thousands. You'll need approximately 80 tiles.

8 **To tile roof,** melt another 1/2 packet of chocolate melts as before. Spread over one roof piece to cover, then, working quickly, cover with tiles. Using chocolate as glue, assemble chimney pieces, then attach chimney to second roof piece. Spread remaining chocolate over second roof piece, avoiding chimney, then cover with remaining tiles.

9 **To assemble house,** melt remaining 1½ packets of chocolate melts as before. Fill a piping bag, then refill as needed. (Alternatively, spoon into a small zip-lock bag and snip corner. Return chocolate to low heat to re-warm, if necessary.) Cool slightly.
• Using melted chocolate as glue, attach long shutters to front downstairs windows, then attach shorter shutters to all other windows. Attach a second set of shutters to the centre of each side window. Attach eave, side supports and door to the front of house (use small objects, such as bottle tops, to support pieces while chocolate sets).
• Using melted chocolate as glue, decorate chimney and all sides of house with assorted lollies.
• On a platter, prop walls up so they are close to their final position (ask someone to hold in position or use weighted boxes or bottles). Pipe a generous amount of chocolate along edges of walls where they meet. Press walls together to seal, then firmly prop between boxes to hold in place while setting. Run a finger over seam of chocolate to spread evenly and to seal any gaps. Pipe chocolate over top edges of walls and attach roof pieces, sealing with plenty of chocolate. Attach licorice ropes along roof eaves. The house will last for up to 2 weeks.

TIP **Use a mix of lollies** to decorate, such as jellies, jubes, bullets and lollipops.

Michael's
STEAK & OYSTERS

This dish put Michael into the lead after the mystery box race – he based it on the flavours of a steak and oyster pie. George was impressed – if he was served this in a restaurant he'd 'talk about it the next day'. Michael also scored a 9 from Gary for this 'perfectly cooked steak and crisp oysters in tempura batter'.

200g Jerusalem artichokes, peeled, thinly sliced
2 x 180g rib-eye steaks
1 tbs extra virgin olive oil
Vegetable oil, to deep-fry
Thinly sliced baby radishes and parsley cress, to serve
BATTERED OYSTERS
50g (1/3 cup) plain flour
2 tsp white wine vinegar
8 oysters

THYME CREME FRAICHE
60g (1/4 cup) crème fraîche
1 sprig thyme, leaves chopped
1 tbs white wine vinegar
SAUCE
1 tbs extra virgin olive oil
20g butter
1 eschalot, thinly sliced
1 small clove garlic, thinly sliced
2 sprigs thyme

1 sprig rosemary
250ml (1 cup) veal stock
BUTTERED BABY VEGETABLES
1 bunch purple baby carrots, trimmed, peeled
1 bunch yellow baby carrots, trimmed, peeled
50g peas
20g butter

1 Cook artichokes in boiling salted water for 3 minutes. Drain, spread out on a tray and refrigerate until needed.

2 For battered oysters, stir together flour, vinegar and 60ml (1/4 cup) water to make a batter the consistency of pouring cream. Season with salt and pepper. Set aside for 15 minutes.

3 For thyme crème fraîche, whisk together all ingredients.

4 To make sauce, heat oil and butter in a small saucepan over medium heat and cook eschalot and garlic for 3 minutes or until softened. Add thyme, rosemary and stock and bring to the boil; cook for 10 minutes or until reduced by half. Strain; keep warm.

5 Rub steaks with olive oil and season with salt. Heat a heavy-based frying pan over high heat and cook steaks for 3 minutes each side for medium–rare, turning once. Transfer to a warm plate, cover loosely with foil and leave to rest for 10 minutes.

6 For buttered baby vegetables, blanch baby carrots in boiling water for 3 minutes or until just tender. Blanch peas for 1 minute; drain. Melt butter in a deep frying pan over medium–high heat and cook vegetables, tossing, for 5 minutes or until tender. Season with salt and keep warm.

7 Fill a deep-fryer or large saucepan one-third full with vegetable oil and heat over medium heat to 180°C (see cooking notes, page 264). Deep-fry Jerusalem artichokes in 2 batches for 4 minutes or until crisp and golden brown. Drain on paper towel and season with salt.

8 Slice steak and arrange on plates with thyme crème fraîche, oysters, Jerusalem artichokes and buttered baby vegetables. Drizzle with a little sauce and scatter with radishes and cress.

Michael's
VANILLA-POACHED LOBSTER

CARAMELISED FENNEL
4 baby fennel bulbs, quartered,
   cored
2 tbs Pernod
60ml (¼ cup) olive oil
40g butter
FENNEL CREAM
30g butter
1 large fennel bulb, grated
60ml (¼ cup) cream, whipped

VANILLA-POACHED LOBSTER
4 green lobster tails, blanched
   for 1 minute, meat removed
300g clarified butter
1 vanilla bean, split, seeds
   scraped
PENCIL LEEKS
50g butter
12 pencil leeks,* trimmed

CHAMPAGNE SAUCE
125ml (½ cup) champagne
1 eschalot, diced
125ml (½ cup) fish stock
1 tbs champagne vinegar
PUFFED WILD RICE
100ml olive oil
25g wild rice

1 **For caramelised fennel,** heat a saucepan of water to 85°C on a thermometer (see cooking notes, page 264). Place fennel, Pernod, pinch of salt and 1 tbs oil in a snap-lock sandwich bag. Expel all air and seal tightly. Place in pan and cook for 35 minutes or until softened, keeping temperature constant throughout cooking. Plunge bag into iced water to stop cooking.

2 **To make fennel cream,** melt butter in a saucepan over medium heat. Add grated fennel, 50ml water and a pinch of salt. Cook, covered, for 20 minutes or until very soft, then purée until smooth. Press through a fine sieve, fold in cream and season with salt.

3 **For vanilla-poached lobster,** heat a large saucepan of water to 60°C on a thermometer. Divide tail meat, clarified butter and vanilla seeds between 2 snap-lock sandwich bags. Expel all air and seal tightly. Place in pan and cook for 12 minutes, keeping temperature constant throughout cooking. Remove from water and rest for 5 minutes before serving.

4 **For pencil leeks,** melt butter with 50ml water and a pinch of salt in a large frying pan over medium heat. Add leeks and cook, turning occasionally, for 5 minutes or until tender.

5 **To make champagne sauce,** put champagne and eschalot in a saucepan over high heat and bring to the boil; cook for 3 minutes or until reduced by two-thirds. Place fish stock in a small saucepan and bring to the boil over high heat; cook for 3 minutes or until reduced by half. Strain champagne into fish stock and add vinegar. Cook over medium–high heat for 3 minutes or until reduced by half. Season to taste.

6 **For puffed wild rice,** heat oil in a saucepan until very hot and cook wild rice for 10–20 seconds or until puffed. Strain oil and drain puffed rice on paper towel. Season with salt.

7 **To finish caramelised fennel,** heat butter and remaining oil in a frying pan over medium–high heat and cook fennel for 4 minutes or until caramelised.

8 **To serve,** spoon fennel cream onto plates. Slice lobster tails and place on top. Add pencil leeks and caramelised fennel, spoon sauce around and scatter with puffed rice.

TIP **Pencil leeks** are baby leeks, about the size of spring onions.

Kate's
QUAIL WITH ROASTED GARLIC CUSTARD

10 quail
80g clarified butter, melted
Parsley cress and chopped
 roasted hazelnuts, to serve
MOUSSE
2 tbs extra virgin olive oil
2 eschalots, finely chopped
2 chicken livers
1 egg white, lightly beaten

1 tbs thickened cream
JUS
2 tbs olive oil
2 chicken wings, jointed
1 onion, diced
1 carrot, diced
1 stalk celery, diced
1 leek, sliced
250ml (1 cup) white wine

375ml (1¹/2 cups) chicken stock
GARLIC CUSTARD
2 bulbs garlic
1 tbs extra virgin olive oil
250ml (1 cup) milk
60ml (¹/4 cup) pouring cream
2 egg yolks
1 whole egg

1 Remove all meat from 2 quail and chop for mousse. Reserve all bones and off-cuts from quail.

2 Cut legs, wings and necks from 4 quail and cut meat from legs for mousse; remove back halves, leaving 2 breast pieces on the bone.

3 Debone remaining 4 quail, removing wing tips, and open out flat without tearing skin.

4 To make mousse, heat olive oil in a small frying pan over low–medium heat and cook eschalots for 3 minutes or until soft. Add livers and cook for 2 minutes over medium heat. Set aside. Process quail meat for mousse with eschalot, liver, egg white and ¹/2 tsp salt until smooth; add cream and process again. Press through a fine sieve, spoon into a piping bag and refrigerate.

5 To make jus, heat olive oil in a frying pan over medium heat and cook quail off-cuts, bones and chicken wings for 5 minutes or until caramelised. Add onion, carrot, celery and leek and cook, stirring occasionally, for 5 minutes or until well browned. Deglaze pan with wine and cook over medium–high heat for 3 minutes or until reduced by three-quarters. Add stock, bring to the boil, reduce heat and simmer for 8 minutes or until reduced by two-thirds. Season and strain.

6 To make ballotines, lay 1 deboned quail flat on plastic wrap on a chopping board. Pipe a 2cm-wide line of mousse down centre of quail and roll up in plastic wrap into a log. Secure at both ends and wrap in another layer of plastic wrap. Repeat with remaining deboned quails.

7 Heat a large saucepan of water to just below simmer (73°C on a thermometer). Add quail ballotines and poach for 35 minutes. Remove and leave for 5 minutes before unwrapping. Heat clarified butter in a frying pan over low heat and cook ballotines for 5 minutes or until golden brown. Rest for 10 minutes.

8 Meanwhile, to make garlic custard, preheat oven to 200°C. Cut garlic bulbs in half crosswise, drizzle with oil and bake for 15 minutes or until tender. Heat milk and cream in a small pan, add garlic, turn off heat and leave for 15 minutes. Whisk yolks and egg until pale; gradually whisk in milk mixture. Season and strain. Grease four 125ml (¹/2-cup) ramekins and line with baking paper. Place in a roasting pan and pour in boiling water to reach halfway up ramekins. Cover with foil and bake for 8 minutes or until just set.

9 Place quail breasts on an oven tray, brush with clarified butter and sprinkle with salt. Bake for 6–8 minutes or until cooked but still pink. Rest for 5 minutes, then cut off the bone to give 8 single breasts. Serve sliced ballotine with roasted quail breasts and garlic custard. Drizzle with jus and sprinkle plate with hazelnuts and cress.

Cooking Notes

Blanch To blanch is to very briefly par-cook. Green vegetables such as beans or asparagus can be dropped into boiling water, cooked or left to stand for 1–2 minutes, then refreshed in iced water to stop the cooking process. This preserves their colour and texture, while taking away the raw flavour.

Blind bake To cook a pastry shell before filling. Line the uncooked pastry with baking paper, extending it well over the sides. Fill with dried beans, uncooked rice or baking weights. Cook for the time instructed, then remove the paper and weights and cook again, as instructed, until the pastry is golden and cooked. When blind baking pastry, you may be instructed to dock it. This simply means to prick the base with a fork to prevent air pockets forming under the pastry during cooking.

Blowtorch A gas-fuelled torch bought from kitchenware shops. This is small and easy to use and gives a good finish to a brulée or meringue, as heat can be directed to one area without affecting the rest of the dish.

Caramelisation The process of cooking sugar until it dissolves and turns golden. This also refers to achieving a desirable brown colour on foods, giving a good indication of flavour development.

Dariole mould A small, usually metal, dish in which individual puddings or desserts can be baked or steamed. Plastic dariole moulds are also available for desserts that are set by chilling.

Deep-fry Fill a deep-fryer or large saucepan one-third full of oil and heat to the specified temperature. A thermometer is the most accurate measure, but you can test with a small cube of bread. At 160°C, bread takes 2½ minutes to turn golden; at 170°C, 1 minute; at 180°C, 35 seconds; at 190°C, 30 seconds.

Deglaze To add liquid such as wine, stock or vinegar to a pan after cooking meat or vegetables. The liquid lifts any caramelised particles from the pan, adding to the flavour of the finished dish or sauce.

French-trim To scrape all meat and sinew from a meat bone for presentation. Lamb racks or cutlets are often prepared in this way. You can French bones yourself or ask your butcher to do it for you.

Gelatine Comes in sheet or powdered form. Professionals will choose the sheets, as they have a neutral taste, give clear jellies a beautiful appearance and are less likely to cause problems during preparation. They are available from specialist food shops and some delis. Use the weight and strength asked for in the recipe (i.e. gold- or titanium-strength).

Grinding & crushing Spices are often roasted and ground before use. If you don't have a mortar and pestle, use a food processor for grinding. Alternatively, seal spices in a sandwich bag and crush by hitting with a rolling pin or the flat side of a meat mallet.

Julienne To cut into julienne is to cut a food (usually a vegetable) into uniform matchstick-shaped pieces.

Micro cress, herbs or greens Used as a garnish, these are very small plants, usually harvested when the first two leaves appear. Buy them in punnets from greengrocers and nurseries. Use scissors to snip the stems, rather than pulling them out of the punnet.

Non-reactive When marinating foods, always use a dish made from a non-reactive material, such as glass or ceramic, which will not be affected by any acidic ingredients in the marinade (wine, vinegar or citrus juice). Stainless-steel bowls are fine for use, but other metals can cause an unpleasant flavour to develop in the food.

Onions You will find several different varieties referred to:
• Onions – the brown variety
• Red onions
• Spring onions – the long, thin, green variety

- Bulb spring onions – long, thin and green with a white bulb at the end
- Eschalots – the small sweet variety with golden-coloured skin, also called French shallots
- Asian red eschalots – the small sweet variety with pink-red skin, available from Asian grocers.

Pastry
When making pastry, butter is rubbed into flour until the mixture resembles coarse breadcrumbs. Use fingertips only – they are cooler than the palms of your hands. This can be done in a food processor, then liquid (such as water or egg) added and pulsed in short bursts until the mixture forms moist clumps. The dough is turned out, gathered together and rolled out as required. Always take care not to over-handle pastry: this causes shrinkage and a tough texture.

Pin-bone
To remove small bones from fish. When preparing a side of salmon, for example, run your fingers along the flesh from tail to head to feel for the tiny bones. Remove them with tweezers.

Preparing prawns
First remove the head. Peel off the shell with the legs and, if removing the tail, squeeze and pull it gently from the body. To 'devein', using a sharp knife, score down the back to expose the dark vein (the digestive tract) and pull it out. To remove without cutting the prawn, carefully pull out from the head end.

Quenelle
Refers to an oval shape, usually used for presentation of cream, ice-cream or mousse. To make a quenelle, use two spoons that have been dipped in hot water. Scoop up some of the mixture in one spoon, then transfer gently from spoon to spoon to form a neat oval shape.

Seasoning
Unless stated otherwise, to season means to add sea salt and freshly ground black pepper to taste.

Sous-vide
A method of cooking. Food is vacuum-sealed in plastic and cooked in water at a low temperature. In restaurant kitchens an appliance regulates the temperature. At home you will need to carefully monitor with a sugar thermometer.

Temperatures
- All oven temperatures are for conventional, non-fan-forced ovens. If you are using a fan-forced oven, set the temperature to 20°C lower than stated in the recipe.
- Use a cooking thermometer to measure the temperature of oil when deep-frying. These thermometers are used for accuracy when making sugar syrups and other types of toffee work. You can also use them to ensure the correct temperature for poaching and when making confit.
- When cooking large cuts of meat, such as lamb rumps or beef fillets, use a meat thermometer to measure the internal temperature of the meat to avoid under- or over-cooking.

Vanilla
Three main forms of vanilla are used in recipes:
- 'Vanilla bean' is vanilla in its purest form – to use, split the bean lengthwise and scrape out the seeds. Often, both seeds and scraped bean are added to a sauce for flavour, with the bean being removed later
- 'Vanilla extract' is from vanilla beans in an alcoholic base
- 'Vanilla bean paste' is derived from vanilla beans and bought in jars – 1 tsp is equivalent to the seeds of 1 vanilla bean.

Wagyu
A breed of cattle that is known for its desirably marbled meat. When cooked, the marbling ensures a moist, juicy result. Wagyu is expensive and can be substituted with good-quality beef.

Weights & sizes
- For accuracy, it is always better to weigh ingredients rather than use cup measures, particularly when baking.
- 1 tablespoon (tbs) holds 20ml or 4 teaspoons (tsp).
- Fruits and vegetables are medium-sized unless specified.
- Unless specified, all eggs used are 59g (extra large).

Zest
This is the finely grated (unless otherwise specified) rind of citrus fruit. Wash any fruit well before grating and avoid the bitter white pith just below the rind. Zest contains highly aromatic oils that give flavour and fragrance to foods.

F

fairytale gingerbread house 254

fennel
  fennel & carrot salad 236
  fennel & crab salad with garlic crème fraîche 120
  fennel salad 158
  fennel, scallop & chorizo salad 64

fig & eggplant braise with flatbread & yoghurt dressing 176

fig & pistachio frozen baklava 174

fish and seafood
  black pepper ocean trout with green mango & spanner crab salad 78
  confit ocean trout with Asian apple salad 160
  crab & fennel salad with garlic crème fraîche 120
  fish stock 94
  garden of marron 90
  green mango & spanner crab salad 78
  lobster bisque with scallops 180
  moules frites 42
  salmon tartare with soft-boiled quail eggs 68
  salt & pepper prawns with lime aïoli 60
  scallop, chorizo & fennel salad 64
  scampi with chilli garlic butter & pineapple salsa 66
  sesame-crusted coral trout 218
  slow-roasted bream in white wine with dill & parsley butter 30
  spiced flounder & scampi with curry sauce 226
  steak & oysters 258
  tea-smoked salmon with orange vinaigrette 212
  Thai-braised Murray cod with crisp chilli & garlic relish 108
  Thai prawn curry 130
  vanilla-poached lobster 260
  W.A. seafood stew 94

flatbread 176

flounder, spiced, & scampi with curry sauce 226

flourless chocolate cake 46

French toast with orange rosewater syrup & figs 132

fried rice 76

G

ganache, chocolate 82, 148

ganache icing 114

garden of marron 90

garden vegetables in an egg net 92

garlic bread 30

garlic crème fraîche 120

garlic wasabi cream 218

gelato, vanilla bean 80

gingerbread house 254

ginger dressing, sweet 34

goat's cheese & caramelised leek tarts 122

goat's cheese tortellini with beetroot 208

goat's curd, preserved lemon 236

Grand Marnier cream 46

grape salad 242

gratin, creamy potato 110

green bean curry 206

gremolata, mint 22

guava sorbet 96

H

harissa lamb, tapas 106

harissa lamb with fennel & carrot salad 236

Hayden Quinn
  braised pork belly with pickled vegetables & sticky rice balls 138
  lobster bisque with scallops 180
  moules frites 42
  scampi with chilli garlic butter & pineapple salsa 66
  sesame-crusted coral trout 218

herb salad 216

herb sauce 194

Heston Blumenthal
  perfection burger 124
  triple-cooked chips 126

honeycomb 32, 248

honey-thyme custard 192

I

ice-cream
  chocolate ice-cream sandwich 246
  coconut ice-cream 58
  Kahlua ice-cream 170
  'Quay' coffee & cardamom 252
  vanilla bean gelato 80

icing
  coffee buttercream 44
  ganache icing 114
  passionfruit icing 232

J

Jay Huxley
  garden of marron 90
  scallop, chorizo & fennel salad 64

K

Kahlua ice-cream 170

Kahlua mousse 252

Kate Bracks
  almond-stuffed squab with parsnip purée 216
  apple pie with vanilla custard 182
  Aussie beef burgers with cheese & caramelised onions 62
  caramelised pumpkin cake 234
  chocolate ice-cream sandwich 246
  quail with roasted garlic custard 262
  'Quay' coffee & cardamom 252
  raspberry & white chocolate puddings with Kahlua ice-cream 170
  retro coffee cake with sticky apples 44
  spiced flounder & scampi with curry sauce 226
  vanilla bean gelato 80

Korean rice burger 140

koupes, lamb, with tzatziki 142

Kumar Pereira
  baklava 50

HarperCollins*Publishers*

First published in Australia in 2011 by HarperCollins*Publishers* Australia Pty Limited
ABN 36 009 913 517 harpercollins.com.au
13/201 Elizabeth St, Sydney, NSW 2000
31 View Road, Glenfield, Auckland 0627, New Zealand

This edition copyright HarperCollins*Publishers* Australia Pty Limited 2011
Published under licence from FremantleMedia Australia Pty Ltd

MasterChef© 2011 Shine (Aust) Pty Ltd. MasterChef is a trademark of Shine (Aust) Pty Ltd.
Licensed by Shine 360°. All rights reserved.

MasterChef® was produced by FremantleMedia Australia Pty Ltd for Network Ten based on the format
owned by Reveille LLC dba ShineReveille

Photography copyright © News Magazines Pty Limited 2011
Recipes copyright © Shine (Aust) Pty Ltd / individual contributors 2011
Other text copyright © News Magazines Pty Limited 2011

National Library of Australia Cataloguing-in-Publication data:
Masterchef: the cookbook. Series 3.
9780732291877(pbk.)
Includes index. Masterchef (Television program) Cooking, Australian.
641.5994

Writer and editor: **Jane Price**

Designer and art director: **Annette Fitzgerald**

Food editor: **Tracy Rutherford**

Food photography: **Jeremy Simons**

Additional photography: **Steve Brown;
Chris Chen; Ben Dearnley; Brett Stevens**

Stylists: **Kristine Duran-Thiessen; Berni Smithies**

Additional styling: **Amber Keller**

Food preparation: **Julie Ballard**

Series photography: **Stuart Bryce**

Editor-in-chief: **Trudi Jenkins**

Creative director: **Scott Cassidy**

Food director: **Sophia Young**

Nigella Lawson's roast beef, Yorkshire pudding and horseradish sauce recipes are taken from *Feast*;
creamy potato gratin recipe is taken from *Nigella Bites*; red velvet cupcakes recipe is taken from
Kitchen. Nigella Lawson's *Feast, Nigella Bites* and *Kitchen* are published by Chatto & Windus,
part of The Random House Group UK.

The publisher wishes to thank the following for their generosity in supplying props and kitchenware
for this book: Bison Australia (bisonhome.com); Funkis (funkis.com); Georg Jensen (georgjensen.com.
au); Hub Furniture (hubfurniture.com.au); Object Gallery (object.com.au); Royal Doulton; Space
Furniture and Design (spacefurniture.com); Top3 by Design.
All meat supplied by Craig Cook's Prime Quality Meats, Northbridge, NSW

Cover design by **Matt Stanton, HarperCollins Design Studio.** Back cover images by **Stuart Bryce.**

Colour reproduction by Graphic Print Group, Adelaide.
Printed and bound in China by RR Donnelley on 128gsm matt art